The Inner Parent

Susan Isaacs and Marti Keller

THE
INNER
PARENT

Raising Ourselves,
Raising Our Children

New York and London
Harcourt Brace Jovanovich

Requests for permission to make copies of any part
of the work should be mailed to:
Permissions, Harcourt Brace Jovanovich, Inc.
757 Third Avenue, New York, N.Y. 10017

Printed in the United States of America

Library of Congress Cataloging in Publication Data
Isaacs, Susan.
The inner parent.

1. Parenting—United States—Psychological aspects.
2. Self-actualization (Psychology)   3. Child development.
I. Keller, Marti, joint author.   II. Title.
HQ755.8.I82   649'.1   78-22256
ISBN 0-15-144423-4

First edition
B C D E

To my beloved teachers,
Murshida and Marge.
SUSAN ISAACS

To Meg and Dorie,
whose loving care of my children
allowed me to work on this manuscript.
MARTI KELLER

Acknowledgments

We extend our sincere thanks and appreciation to the many people who have counseled and supported us during the years of work on this book:

We thank all the parents we interviewed for graciously allowing us to visit their lives.

We thank the professionals who so generously shared their knowledge and experience: Robert Royeton for reading the chapter on personal myths and fantasies, and Robert Munson for reading the chapter on values and helping to refine them; Phillip Mitchell for sharing his class materials on needs and his concept of Mistaken Certainties; Betty Cohen from Bananas child care referral switchboard for her insights into hot-line counseling; Mary Bauman from the California State University at Hayward graduate program in marriage and family counseling for sharing sources for the crisis chapter; and Carolyn Robertson for allowing us to observe and participate in her class on mothering.

We wish to thank Louise Sullivan for the many hours she spent typing the manuscript; Allison Van Dyke for compiling and typing the bibliographic notes; Hank Mindlin for his brainstorming; Ira Deitrick for his wise counsel; Alain Youell for providing recreation and inspiration during the editing process; and most especially Anne Coleman for her courageous belief in the worth of the book.

We are also indebted to Lois Murphy, Irene Kane, and Mary Lane for their willingness to look at the manuscript and help us in the final stages of its development, and throughout to Brian Dumaine, our editor, for his warm interest and gentle guidance.

We thank our parents for their roles in our growth and their faith in our efforts, our husbands for their help and encouragement, and our children for giving us the experience of raising them, and in the process raising ourselves.

Susan Isaacs
Walnut Creek, California

Marti Keller
Kensington, California

January 1979

Contents

Foreword

A deep revolution has begun in America.

Not a revolution intent on changing the economic system, the social structure, or our form of governance; it is a revolution that aims to transform the very source of the consciousness and selfhood which give rise to life in society.

From the point of view of physical comforts, our culture has attained the highest standard of living of any society in recorded history. This has been possible because we have spent centuries directing our attention outward, using our reason and senses to understand and subdue—or at least manage—the laws governing matter. The triumphs of modern technology are an everyday witness to the achievements of this outward orientation.

But the emphasis, indeed overemphasis, of our culture on technique, reason, physical comforts, and outward (that is, behavioral) concerns has extracted its price: a loss of conscious connection with the deeper—inner—levels of ourselves, the parts that are nourished by intuition, intimacy, community, and a sense of purpose and meaningfulness. We may have succeeded in our quest for material well-being, but that success has brought with it a profound lesson: material well-being does not necessarily bring happiness or peace or satisfaction. The quality of life is not measured by the quantity of goods available at the market. Our preoccupation with the outer worlds of matter, of technique, of power, fame, and wealth, has left an inner hunger, a deep restlessness.

There are many who have recognized the inevitability of this crisis and have heralded the need for a deep revolution—a revolution to redress the balance between the outer and the inner, reason and intuition, material prosperity and spiritual understanding. Carl Jung's *Modern Man in Search of a Soul* is one such book which, recognizing the crisis, echoes concerns raised already a century ago by Emerson, Thoreau, and Whitman. More recently, Viktor Frankl's *Man's Search for Meaning*, Charles Reich's *The Greening of America*, Theodore Roszak's *The Making of a Counter Culture*, and Willis Harman's *Changing Images of Man* all call for us to turn inward that we may reclaim for ourselves and for those whom we love the rights and joys of personal self-sufficiency, intuition, and spiritual community even in the midst of material well-being.

The Inner Parent is a book that reflects this same change of consciousness, this deep revolution within our culture. More important, by bringing principles of that revolution to bear upon the all-important and inescapably practical subject of parenting, this book not merely mirrors the change but becomes an active instrument of it. For that reason it is a unique book and an important book.

There are at least five reorienting principles of the deep revolution. *The Inner Parent* applies each of these to our experience as parents.

1. *An emphasis on process:* Because matter usually presents itself to us as static, our preoccupation with the outer life has led many of us—including psychologists, sociologists, and educators—to view ourselves, others, and the roles that we assume throughout life as similarly static. It is only in the past few years, with Levenson's *The Seasons of a Man's Life* and Gail Sheehy's *Passages*, that there has been a growing recognition that inner

growth and change—that is, inner process—continue even after outer, physical growth and change have largely ceased. In many respects, *The Inner Parent* begins where *Passages* leaves off: recognizing adulthood as a process, Ms. Isaacs and Ms. Keller reveal how, in giving birth to a child, a couple at the same time give birth to themselves as parents. This child-birth is parent-birth, the beginning of a process of growth for the parents which is just as dynamic, living, and challenging as the developmental process is for the child. Moreover, whereas most books on parenting define the joys, stresses, and strains of parenthood largely in relation to the stages of development of the children (for example, how to handle toilet training, the first day of school, the new sibling, and so on), *The Inner Parent* traces the major phases/tasks/processes of parenting as aspects of adult development, thus exploring for the first time the psychology of *parent* development.

2. *An emphasis on intuition and self-sufficiency:* Process means living change, and living change means that each moment of the present is a living moment, a new moment, a new situation, a new challenge. And what that means is that those of us who wish to participate in the deep revolution cannot count on precepts, rules, laws, or principles to guide us through our life experiences. For a rule is static—it may seem to provide direction, certainty, and surety, but when applied to life, rules actually provide only false security and misdirection. Why? Because rules are lifeless; they are not alive to the uniqueness of the moment, to the possibility and call of the process. They work only when the present is like the past and the future like the present. They straitjacket the heart. Thus the deep revolution—and *The Inner Parent* as an application of that consciousness revolution to parenting—is a call to intuition, to trusting oneself and one's own responsiveness to the ongoing processes of life. Not experts, not rules, not guidebooks, not even one's own past experiences with parents or friends are as important as the clear perception

of the living moment. And as no one can live that moment for us, so no one can see that moment for us. What Ms. Isaacs and Ms. Keller offer are pointers to help us attune ourselves to our own intuition.

3. *An emphasis on community:* Though the deep revolution emphasizes self-sufficiency based on intuition, it does not make the mistake of isolating the individual or of separating us from a sense of community. On the contrary, the process that we are in the middle of—the process of growth, maturation, increasing responsiveness, and increasing responsibility—is not different for each of us. There is, finally, only One Process, and each of us is conscious of and participates in that One Process as best we can. Thus the deep revolution does not place the individual in isolation to fend for herself or himself in competition or separateness. Rather it produces *recognition* and *relief:* recognition that we are all in this process, this life, this experience of growing together; and relief that we can turn to one another for understanding, sympathy, and encouragement. The interviews in each chapter of *The Inner Parent* convey these states of recognition and relief to each parent or parent-to-be: we recognize ourselves in the experiences, crises, joys, and doubts of others; we experience relief that our inner processes of trying to be or become parents are shared by others—we are not alone.

4. *An emphasis on values:* The world of matter presents itself as a world of objectivity, a world of "facts," a valueless world. So much of modern psychology, sociology, education, philosophy—even religion—has been influenced by this outward view that many of us have lost touch with the living source of values within us. The deep revolution is a reminder that values are essential, inextricably bound up to every thought, every judgment, every decision. Not that we all value the same things; but it is impossible not to value something—and some things more than other things. Because it is the inner life, the life of feeling and intuition, which spawns our values, the deep revolution

awakens us to the part of us that gives rise to our values. And *The Inner Parent* reminds us that more than anything else, to parent is to communicate values.

5. *An emphasis on action:* The deep revolution—and the inner awakening that it heralds—is not a matter of thought and theory or of talk and argument. It is a matter of action —of applying the insights and truths we have discovered and understood about ourselves, including ourselves as parents, to the everyday texture of our lives. *The Inner Parent,* like any other handbook of the deep revolution, must be lived if it is to share its power. It is not a report on research (though it reports on research); it is not a theoretical study (though it includes theory); it is not a book for entertainment (though it is entertaining)—rather, it is a call to action, a call to experiment in one's own life with the processes of parenthood in order better to understand ourselves, and better to serve our children and one another.

The Inner Parent is a pivotal book. It follows in the stream of Elisabeth Kubler-Ross's *On Death and Dying,* Gail Sheehy's *Passages,* Arthur Young's *The Reflexive Universe,* Meher Baba's *Discourses,* and those few other books that see life as an inner process requiring intuition as well as reason, recognition and community as well as individuality, self-sufficiency as well as expertise, action as well as thought. It is special, however—and important— because Ms. Keller and Ms. Isaacs have applied the best understanding of the deep revolution to the experience of parenting, and in so doing they have brought to our awareness a whole new orientation for understanding ourselves and, together with our children, creating our future.

Pascal M. Kaplan, Ph.D.
Dean, School of General Studies
John F. Kennedy University
Orinda, California

December 1978

Preface

Parenting, as it is—not as one expert or another feels it should be—can be a rich opportunity for discovery and growth.

As professionals in the field of early child development, and as mothers of young children, we have been concerned about the disparity between the frozen image of parenthood which results from technical approaches to child rearing and the fluid and individualized nature of the parent-child relationship.

This book began in the fall of 1972. At that time Susan Isaacs created the Early Learning Center in San Francisco, California. This center was a source of information and ideas about activities for babies and toddlers and, more importantly, a place where parents, mainly of first-borns, could talk to one another about their experiences—articulate feelings, share problems, test theories, and dispel preconceptions.

Marti Keller joined the staff of the Early Learning Center that winter as a specialist in movement and creative play activities for young children. She, like Susan, was a parent herself, new in the role and fresh in her journey.

Susan had worked with many preschool parent groups before, but this was her first opportunity to lead group discussions with parents of even younger children. Neither of us had been aware of *how early* parents experienced anxiety about their methods of child rearing. Although we ourselves had also worried about the job we were doing as mothers and had compared it with the expert advice popular that year, we had not realized how widespread was this profound concern with and dependency on outside sources of information. We were struck by the acute sense of isolation felt by many of the mothers in our center. Out of this isolation and insecurity came a critical need to talk about the issues of parenting.

During twice-weekly discussions with the parents in the program, we found that these mostly middle-class, professional women viewed parenthood as a complex skill or series of skills—like the steps involved in driving a car —that a person might or might not master. Implicit in these informal conversations was the assumption that there was a technique tailor-made to any problem or crisis; one only had to search among the professional guidebooks to find the match.

Sprinkled through the discussions were references to different popular authorities on child development: "I'm just going to stick to Dodson," or, "Salk has the best answers." As one adviser failed to provide satisfactory answers, another appeared to take his place.

While these parents seemed outwardly dependent on the books they were reading, the group discussions eventually became a source of reinforcement for their own common sense and awareness of inner resources. Even when confronted by examples of their own effective problem solving, parents found it difficult to let go of their cultural bias that learning happens in pedantic ways. What we saw here, and had seen in other parent groups, was the parents' emerging conviction that learning has little to do with assimilating book materials. Individual insights about family situations and parent-child relationships sparked the solutions and growth.

It also became clear in the course of a year's relationship with this group of parents that they shared—like their children—common processes of growth and development. This book describes these processes and offers some guidelines for increasing our awareness of them. Parents and nonparents alike will find these elements of growth helpful in understanding their relationships with their families, whether their own children or their parents.

We have talked about the hidden myths that color our perceptions of ourselves and our children. We have examined the ways we choose to meet our needs and how we can balance them with those of our family. We have described the many identities of adulthood and demonstrated some of the expectations parents have of parenthood.

This book offers approaches to defining and clarifying our beliefs as they affect our relationships with our families. And it details the warning signs of personal crisis, suggesting how we can use these signals as routes to recovery and growth.

Our experience with the parent group at the Early Learning Center demonstrated to us the need for a book recording parents' real words, their joys as well as their frustrations, and, most important, the insights they share about their own growth as adults. This book could serve as a basis for ongoing discussion groups, or as a resource for an individual groping with these same issues.

Our conversations with parents extended to a widespread population—still mainly composed of middle-class white parents, but also reaching people from diverse cultural backgrounds, income levels, and family situations.

At one point early on it seemed tempting to interview famous parents: Joan Baez, Jane Fonda, Robert Redford, sculptress Ruth Asawa. How did they sort out their values and priorities? Who were their role models? What did they want for their children? Although this tack was tempting, it also seemed inappropriate. If we were after an accurate picture of parenthood, then it was critical that we select parents in the mainstream, not from the glamorous fringes of this society.

During the two years of interviewing and of writing this book, we were fortunate to come in contact with a fascinating, searching group of people—American parents in the last part of this century—who, more than ever before, are participating in a social and cultural evolution.

We found their individual stories rich and important. We feel sure you will agree.

The Inner Parent

I. The Joy of Parenting

No one can acquire for another—not one,
Not one can grow for another—not one.[1]

The best thing to read when trying to raise a child is the child. Maybe it is even more important that we learn to read ourselves. Most of the time when we try to read books that tell us how to deal with problems, we get problems. Problems are contagious. Look how easily our children catch them from us.[2]

The expert with the easy answers seems to be encouraging people to expect the very least from themselves. Books that provide lesson plans for fighting or making up in marriage, for disciplining children, for how to be more sexy, are an insult to the intelligence—for no matter how we may be seduced into longing for the simple solution, we know it never works.[3]

Most parenting books start with the premise that the author knows something that the reader does not. This book is based on quite different assumptions: that parents learn most effectively through developing insights into their own experience and by sharing that experience with others; and that the most valuable thing an "expert" can offer is not advice, information, or even techniques, but respect for parents and their power to use their inner resources to give rise to family growth.

Imagine that you are making your way through the

morning paper. The beginning of this article attracts your attention:

PLAN YIELDS BEST CHILDREN
by Daniel A. Haney, Boston AP

The brightest, happiest, most charming children spend their earliest years in remarkably similar ways, researchers say. They listen to adult conversations, roam freely around their homes, and spend a lot of time staring. The study, they say, provides a blueprint for raising terrific kids . . .

Do you go on and read the article? Or does your eye travel down the page to a juicier bit of news? If you are a parent—or hope to be one in the foreseeable future— the chances are that you will read at least the first paragraph and most likely the whole article.

You may read it skeptically; it may even evoke some hostile responses. You may reject the idea proposed by Harvard researcher Burton White that there are, in fact, standard variables that go into making the brightest, happiest, most charming children. Or you may side with the late Haim Ginott's premise that the qualities of humanity and strength are superior to brightness and charm. You may find yourself caught up in the concept that there might be a plan to produce the best kids. (Why not yours?) Still, whatever your predisposition or response, you will almost certainly feel a need to read this article— or a twinge of guilt if you don't. Why? Because for a contemporary parent or parent-to-be, the problem of raising children is complex enough and produces enough anxiety to make all but the most antiliterate parents seek more written information. When it comes to parenting, information about children is often seen as our number-one resource, our most valuable commodity.

Parents may dismiss the idea of a blueprint for child raising as absurd. However, the very fact that they will feel compelled to read an article like the one above promising master plans for child rearing belies their real interest. Among sophisticated parents, especially, it is fashionable to scoff at the use of formulas for solving the problems of handling one's children. Publicly they dismiss "the expert," who, they say, lacks firsthand experience with children outside his ivory tower. The reality of living with children night and day is enough to poke holes in any theory, parents say. Today it is the vogue to ridicule the child-rearing cookbook written by a master chef of child development, psychiatry, or pediatrics who gives us recipes for the perfect child and the perfect parent.

Perhaps we are still haunted by that image from thirty years ago of the frenzied mother, lacking the confidence and self-esteem, who kept a copy of "Dr. Spock's Bible" on each floor of her house. The stereotype persists today, but the authors are just as likely to be Dr. Ginott or Dr. Thomas Gordon.

But if we are so skeptical about dependence on experts, why is the probability that we will read that newspaper article so high? Why are large-circulation magazines overflowing with articles on how to be a better parent? Why are new books, whose titles are often so similar you can hardly distinguish them, gobbled up as soon as they come off the press? The market for these "how to" books on child rearing is far from shrinking; there are actually more and more of them being published and endlessly discussed.[4]

If there is a difference in the current crop of books, it is that they attempt to focus on more and more subtle nuances of the parenting relationship and on more specific areas of development. Today a broad picture of development is not seen as adequate. There are books focusing on one year of the child's life or on concrete events such as divorce or death. There are books on how to fulfill the role of father, of grandparent. New parental roles and activities are even invented in books on specific kinds of exercise for babies, on yoga for children, on how to teach your preschooler to cook or your baby to read.

Dr. Richard Farson, who has just written a book on parents, names the desire of parents to get information about their children as the country's number-one obsession. "We keep inventing responsibilities for parents . . . our idea of parenthood is that there is a right way to do it. . . . The idea of telling someone else how to love (or how to parent) is absurd."[5]

If, however, we do feel that there is a right way to parent, why don't we just conform to it? The directions are there. The specifications are more than detailed. The answer is—we try. But in spite of the enormous amounts of money and time spent trying to accommodate ourselves to these ideals, there seems to be an eventual—if often unconscious—dissatisfaction with what they provide us. It's not that the techniques don't work. Parents swear by them. But they also say that none of them adequately satisfies their needs for the continual understanding and awareness necessary to meet the day-to-day demands of their roles.

It may be too threatening to admit that no technique, book, or course, no matter how relevant, can fit the unique and changing form of our human relationships. It may be even harder to accept that the basic changes in our personalities and in our approaches to the world do not come from reading books that tell us how to do it. If we admit these things, especially to ourselves, we may have a crisis. Where can we turn?

So we avoid the crisis by trying to conform to the experts' plans for our behavior or by feeling that we will manage to muddle through somehow.

Why has the ever increasing attention to the advice of child care experts failed to help parents care for children with relaxation and confidence? Why if anything has the advice often seemed to create more fear than it allayed. . . . Modern parent education is characterized by the experts pointing out in great detail all the mistakes parents have and might possibly make and substituting scientific knowledge for the tradition of the good old days . . . an unrelieved picture of modern parental behavior, a contrived image of artificial perfection and happiness is held up before parents who valiantly try to reach the ever receding ideal of good parenthood like dogs after a mechanical rabbit.[6]

The anxiety basic to most modern parents has led some of them in recent years to react against current trends in favor of the kind of thinking they imagine to have been common in the past. In keeping with contemporary movements, which stress a back-to-the-earth approach to life, many new parents have rejected the idea of informed parenthood as we have become accustomed to it. They espouse instinct as the answer. They often view reading books about children with suspicion because they "do not want their instincts to be clouded."

When stress and anxiety are high in society, there is often a desire to return to ways of the past, which seem safe and secure. But many people lack the breadth of experience their ancestors had as members of large and extended families. These romanticized forebears at the very least had a great deal to do with babies and children—brothers, sisters, cousins, nephews, and nieces—before they had families of their own. They also lived in a society where there was little confusion about how to raise children. There was a consensus on the values that gave direction to a parent.

So for the modern parent from a typically small nuclear family—a family that has been exposed over the last generation to one of the biggest values shake-ups that we have seen in recently recorded history—relying on instinct may not be the satisfactory answer either.

But where do we go when our parental instincts seem inadequate in preparing us for the total task of parenting?

Many first time mothers prepare themselves far better for childbirth than for the child care that comes afterward. They take classes, exercise, and read technical manuals to prepare for delivery. But it is assumed that when the infant arrives, natural instincts will take over. In reality, the new mother finds she needs a lot of information and especially reassurance. At this point she almost invariably turns to one resource, her mother.[7]

But relationships have changed too. Where Grandmother's advice in the past might have been taken as gospel, new mothers, who want to do things quite differently from the way their parents did, often see advice as interference.

The point is that today most of us come into our roles as parents with only a sketchy understanding of what is involved. In the majority of cases we are not adequately prepared by our experiences as adults, nor by our limited awareness of the unspoken rules, expectations, and patterns that our own childhoods have provided as a model for us. The sad thing is that these internal blueprints influence our thinking and behavior without furnishing us with a clear, updated picture of what we want either for ourselves or for our children. This is not to say that we do not have access to parts of ourselves that help us respond to life on highly intuitive levels. The problem with our internal programs is the same as with those handed to us by the experts: they are not always flexible enough to weather the pace of modern life. In most cases they are simply inadequate.

"The fundamental cause of parental anxiety," argues Harvard psychologist Jerome Kagan, "is a lack of consensus in values. Parenting means implementing a series of decisions about the socialization of your child—what do you do when he cries, when he's aggressive, when he lies, or when he doesn't do well in school. Fifty years ago," he says, "such decisions were easier to make because Americans possessed a common agreement about what good parents should do. . . . In contrast, there is no consensus in America today as to what a child should be like when he is a young adult or what you should do to get him there."[8]

Neither instinct nor generalized information can substitute for that secure conviction, passed on in the past from generation to generation, which furnished the guidelines and goals for rearing children. That inner certainty that allowed generations of citizens to implement and adapt their own value systems to slowly changing ways of life through common goals has been destroyed all but completely in this century because of:

- the decline almost to extinction of the extended family, robbing people of adequate preparenting experience and counsel in their early parenting years;
- the breakdown of the nuclear family through divorce, creating inordinate pressures and responsibilities for one parent and severe economic pressures on both;
- the advent of the single-parent and communal family, resulting in new roles and life-styles for which there are few models;
- the vast increase in the number of working mothers and the changing views of men's and women's roles, putting pressures on families to change in unprecedented ways;
- the lack of respect afforded to caring for children, contributing to parents' seeing their roles as ineffective and meaningless;
- the plaguing of even the early adolescent years with social problems of a variety and scope we could not have imagined two decades ago—alcohol and drug abuse, suicide, the phenomenon of runaways, early sexual activity, and the high incidence of pregnancy with few infants given up for adoption—involving parents of these teenagers in crises that inevitably leave them feeling out of control and overwhelmed;
- the widespread breakdown of religious beliefs and struc-

tures as a source of family solidarity and of agreement on values;
· the ever increasing, unmet need to find out-of-the-home care for children, leaving parents with both a recurring crisis in finding such care and the exposure of their families to new and different value systems if they do;
· the blame that is popularly placed on parents for their seeming ineffectiveness in times of change and rampant family disorganization.

"The things we're trying to cope with today are just more complex than our parents had to deal with," says a director of a family service agency who is himself a father. "Parents have lost control over their families. They feel inadequate and overwhelmed. I know I do."[9]

Where is a parent to turn? When overwhelmed by choices, information, and isolation, whose advice does one choose to follow? We are surrounded by the examples of other parents who have seemingly—by the evidence of their offspring's lives—made bad decisions. It is difficult to find a model whose values we trust—especially if our own values are in confusion.

And in the ongoing confusion, the advice of the expert becomes one of the few, if temporary, comforts to anxious parents, regardless of—and perhaps because of—the impersonality of that support. In fact, parents value the seeming generalness and objectivity of the expert as proof that he or she knows what will happen as the result of standardized procedures. The fact that the expert is a human being too, with personal values and beliefs, rarely enters the parent's mind. It is the objectivity of the written word that convinces us that the expert's experience—even from its ivory tower perspective—is more valuable and certainly more authoritative than our own.

Human values and their relation to all these opinions expressed on child rearing are virtually ignored.[10] It was this faith in objectivity that caused parents to rage at Dr. Spock when it became clear, through his stance on the war in Vietnam and his support of peace demonstrators, that his values and goals were an expression of his individual humanity. Parents felt duped. The fact that he was a human being rather than an abstract source of information led them to blame the product of their former credulity—in this case a whole generation—on him. Yet it never seems to occur to people now that the whole spectrum of writers on child rearing are, like Dr. Spock, people who layer their own writing with personal and unconscious value systems as a foundation for their advice.

Parents have inferred from the example of Dr. Spock that his answers were wrong, rather than simply value-laden. Therefore, they have tried to find someone else with more agreeable answers. Because of their temporary disillusionment (parents still read and benefit from Dr. Spock's advice), people may scoff at the belief in the necessity of an expert as a resource for information and support, but their *feeling* of dependence has hardly diminished.

Although we live in a world full of scientific miracles, and in spite of the claims of many experts in the field, no universal blueprint for good child rearing has ever been produced. And regardless of the desires of all of us who strive to improve the lives of our children and our abilities as parents, it is doubtful that it ever will.

Realizing the dilemma of modern parents who depend so heavily on external sources of information, many authors have advised readers to rely more on their own judgment and common sense. The inherent problem with this is, as Marshall McLuhan once said, that "the medium is the message." Many authors might make statements such as, "No one can know better than a parent what to do for his own child." But the fact that the parent gets this advice from a book is still the real message; you go to a book whose purpose is to convince you to depend on yourself. Parents remain unconvinced.

In all truth, we have presented a one-sided picture. To say that there are anxiety-ridden parents is to describe more accurately the state of our society than the quality of our parents. To portray parents as dependent, confused, and helpless is to ignore one reality for the sake of another. Modern parents are living up to the tasks of being more resourceful than their ancestors needed to be and of creating stability in the midst of change that their ancestors couldn't have imagined.

Modern parents are learning fast that survival depends upon being creative and flexible enough to learn through their own experience and upon seeking out the resources and support of others. The natural childbirth movement too, which has aroused major controversy concerning whether childbirth should be a personalized or a medically standardized experience, has made a definite but subtle impact on the way parents relate to their children. For adults who have worked hard to involve themselves in the exhilarating, intense experience of childbirth, the idea of relying on someone else to advise them on what to do afterward can seem very sterile.

Parents who have prepared for childbirth are often hit with three realizations immediately after the birth of their child: (1) that if they have been prepared for childbirth, they have been grossly underprepared for parenthood; (2) that the relationships and sharing they experienced in their preparatory childbirth classes now seem as valuable as the content of those classes; (3) that if they saw, in childbirth, that they could have some control over the process, why shouldn't that self-determination continue?

The first realization describes an initial crisis of parenting. The second and third are the basis for some of the avenues that modern parents are beginning to explore in order to fulfill their own unique potentials as persons who are parents.

Today more and more parents are attempting to discover what it is *they* believe through an examination of their perceptions, both alone and in the supportive presence of others. They are learning to discover and implement their own values. They are creating and attending groups in their homes, schools, churches, and elsewhere as forums where they can discuss their feelings about children and about how being a parent has changed their feelings toward themselves.

But if parenthood is to regain its qualities of joy and purpose, its positive aspects must find articulation. Now that having children is for most Americans a matter of choice, not chance, perhaps today's parents will develop a new vocabulary to describe the satisfaction of giving life to somebody. Parents are learning to reach out to each other, even when they are strangers. Where the experts have failed, parents have been successful in helping each other.[11]

This consciousness, which focuses on the *parent's perceptions,* is a new arrival on the child-rearing scene. It has helped to bring to awareness the idea that there are stages of development in parenting (as part of adulthood) just as there are in childhood. In the past parents have learned as they moved through the progressive cycles of parenthood—from infancy to independence—that the process itself (even if they didn't have a real grasp of it) worked as a powerful impetus for growth and change. Today we are finding that *focusing on those changes* and what they can teach us can give us an even deeper understanding of ourselves. Along with that realization comes the knowledge that parenthood, if approached creatively, carries all the risks of growth that can make us want to run for safety. Giving up external blueprints and committing ourselves to examine the incomplete ones we carry with us can be a responsibility we may not feel ready to take.

The work of adult life is not easy. As in childhood, each step not only presents new tasks of development but requires a letting go of the techniques that worked before. With each passage some magic must be given up, some cherished illusion of safety and comfortably familiar sense of self must be cast off, to allow for the greater expansion of our own distinctiveness.[12]

Growth implies taking steps that no one else has mapped out for us. It involves being willing to cut our own paths into previously unexplored areas of parenting. This book is designed for exploration. It is not based, as noted in the first paragraph, on the premise that the authors have the "answers" and the reader can learn them. The only answer we provide is the joy which can be gained from engaging in our own growth processes. That's what this book is about: growth and change.

What we as authors have attempted to do is create a focus for looking at and encouraging growth by exploring some of the ways individual parents have viewed their roles and perceptions at particular times. We do not offer these samples of others' experience as answers to parenting problems. We see them as models of how we can be aware of the processes of parenting.

The chapters have been organized to explore specific areas of development in parents rather than specific problems. Most books on parenthood have been organized according to the child's stages of development in order to facilitate the parent's optimum response to the problems and potentials of each age. We feel that for our purposes this system of organzation would be a mistake. We do not dispute the fact that there are common aspects to the developmental cycles that describe children's individual development. We do protest the idea that a parent's growth is defined by these stages.

A mother who has her first child at thirty is a different person and parent from the one she would have been at eighteen. A thirty-year-old mother who had her first child at eighteen and her third child at thirty similarly brings a difference in experience and identity to her role and her relationship with that new baby.

We feel that it is the evolution of our perceptions that allows us to approach parenthood creatively. We believe this is more important than the solutions to day-to-day problems that could be related superficially to a child's particular age or stage.[13] A father who has learned to be in touch with who he is and what his feelings are is more apt to be responsive to the way his child sees himself. A mother who has explored her needs for nurturance and comfort is more able to provide the same for her children regardless of their ages. This awareness contributes more to familial relationships than do answers to specific questions or even methods of discipline, despite what the books on the subject may imply. It also seems important to us for people at different ends of the parenthood cycle to be able to share their perspectives and to learn from one another. The thirty-year-old mother with a new baby and her friend the same age with a twelve-year-old may be experiencing the same identity crisis. To define their growth by the ages of their children would be to say that the birth of our experience coincides with our children's birth.

Many of us have felt, in becoming parents, that our task was to create a product—the child, the adolescent, the adult. Perhaps it is this presumption that has constituted our biggest stumbling block. Intent on the product, we have lost track of the emerging person being packaged. Focusing so exclusively on molding another's growth, we have often forgotten or ignored our own.

In our view, the task of all parents is to create themselves. Our children's growth can follow its own individual path if we permit our capacities for learning and change to serve as a model.

If parents ignore their responsibilities for this growth and awareness, their children, sensing stagnation, will find models and direction outside their parents' jurisdiction. We will never be our children's only teachers, but we can enjoy the responsibility of being their first and most important ones. In addition, life must obviously mean more than being a model for our children. Having a child can affect and alter our course strategically. It is important for us to be aware of that before we make the decision to have children. It can influence our identities, decisions, and life tasks for years on end.

We hope that this book will provide a starting point for focusing on the most neglected and yet important part of parenthood: the opportunities for our own inner development. Toward that end, we have put forth seven dynamic processes. You will probably discover more.

1. Exploring our fantasies: the hidden expectations and aspects of ourselves that we bring to parenting, as seen in Chapter 2, "Seeing Through Our Myths."
2. Reevaluating our ideas about pregnancy and birth, as seen in Chapter 3, "Giving Birth to the Parent."
3. Refocusing our identities: how the process of parenthood influences our definitions of ourselves, as seen in Chapter 4, "Making Room for the Parent Within Us."
4. Sorting our needs: the creative juggling of our needs with the needs of others, as seen in Chapter 5, "Balancing Needs."
5. Recognizing and dealing effectively with problems, as seen in Chapter 6, "Learning from Crisis."
6. Giving voice to our inner parent, as seen in Chapter 7, "Articulating Our Thoughts and Dreams."
7. Discovering and communicating our beliefs to others, as seen in Chapter 8, "Clarifying Our Values."

This book is not a piece of research, a cookbook, or an exhaustive reflection on the feelings and ideas presented either by the people included or by groups in our society. It is a catalyst, we hope, for helping people to see parenthood in a new way. The study of children and how they develop has brought about a whole new age of parenting. However, we have become preoccupied with analysis and a problem-oriented approach to children and parenting that limits our effectiveness as well as our joy. To take a step beyond this limiting vision we must integrate our knowledge, feelings, and expectations into a whole that helps to actualize our own uniqueness.

Coming to terms with yourself means gradually realizing what your expectations for yourself and those around you are, what your needs are, and what the unfinished business of your own growing up seems to be. In the process of developing self-awareness about your expectations, you actually learn all kinds of things.[14]

NOTES

1. Walt Whitman, "A Song of the Rolling Earth," in *The Complete Poetry and Prose of Walt Whitman* (Garden City, N.Y.: Country Life Press, 1948), p. 219.
2. Polly Berrien Berends, *Whole Child, Whole Parent* (New York: Harper's Magazine Press, 1975), p. 219.
3. Eda Le Shan, *The Wonderful Crisis of Middle Age* (New York: David McKay Co., Inc., 1971), p. 11.
4. "On Being an American Parent," *Time* magazine, 1976. U.S. parents lead the world market for books on child rearing, purchasing $20.5 million worth yearly. In addition, parents will pay high prices for techniques delivered by experts in courses, lectures, and groups; some 500,000 parents a year sign up for Parent Effectiveness classes at $60 a shot.
5. From a talk at Palomar College, San Marcos, California, April 1976.
6. Stella Chess, *Your Child Is a Person* (New York: Parallax Publishing Co., Simon & Schuster, 1965), p. 3.
7. AP, Ann Arbor, Michigan.
8. "The Parent Gap," *Newsweek*, September 22, 1975.
9. *Ibid.*
10. Whoever thought about values anyway? It's a word that has changed its functional meaning in a generation. Prior to the sixties our beliefs and attitudes were most often thought to be prescribed by our station in society (the values we ought to have). When our belief system was laid bare by dissent, reaction, and counterreaction, opening us to the perspectives of people previously ignored or unheard, the word *value* suddenly implied a stance—a decision. The idea that values involve a process or processes rather than existing as fixed entities has been made popular by Raths, Harmin, and Simon in *Values and Teaching;* and Simon, Howe, and Kirschenbaum in *Values Clarification.* However, looking at the population as a whole, this is still considered a relatively new approach to decision making.
11. Even in the difficult area of child abuse, parents have proved themselves uniquely successful in helping one another. Parents

Anonymous, an organization started and run exclusively by parents, is one of the only successful organizations for changing child-abusing parents.

12. Gail Sheehy, *Passages: Predictable Crises of Adult Life* (New York: E. P. Dutton, 1975), p. 21.

13. Some models for looking at the process rather than the content of personal growth are found in books on humanistic psychology: the previously mentioned books on values; Erik Erikson's description of eight life stages in *Childhood and Society;* Gail Sheehy's best-seller, *Passages;* and, with specific reference to parents, *The Growth and Development of Mothers,* by Angela Barron McBride.

14. Angela Barron McBride, *The Growth and Development of Mothers* (New York: Harper & Row, 1973), p. 113.

2. Seeing Through Our Myths

Many of us think of fantasy as mere daydreaming, an inviting pastime that may help us escape from the daily rhythm of our lives. If we seek a temporary liberation from our roles and responsibilities, we may indulge in fantasies about sex or food or travel. If we feel we are missing accomplishments, important deeds, or adventure, our fantasies may focus on our performing unrealistic acts or even starting whole new careers. In any case, unless fantasy substitutes for real activity, we tend to think of it as important only for the brief respite it provides us from the demands of reality. Although fantasy may lead to creativity in that it occasionally forms ideas for things we will actually do, enjoy, or generate, we don't usually expect it to exercise much power over the general flow of our lives.

In this chapter we would like you, if only for a brief time, to look at fantasy in a completely different way. As adults—and even more important, as potential or actual parents—we are not interested in the ways fantasy gives us relief from our roles but in the way it actually conditions and guides them. But in order to appreciate this process, you will have to look just for the fun of it on your whole life as being a fantasy—not something unreal or ephemeral, but as a story or a play that you have created and cast yourself in as the star. Think about the decisions you have made about your life—how are they part of the whole drama? Who are the other characters you have chosen? What is the backdrop for your play? Where have you chosen to act it out? What is the drama of your play? Is it a slice of life without much direction? Has someone else handed you the script? What will the climax or at least some of the highlights be?

The important things for you to look at in taking this view of your life as a play are the ways in which you have created the myth you are living. One way you can explore this is to think back to the fantasies you had as a child or an adolescent about your adult life. How many of them have come true? Or, more important, how did your needs and ideals *then*, your aspirations and fears, condition the decisions you made for your life later on? If you can think back this way, you can get a sense, even in quite subtle ways, of how the parts you have written for yourself were created.

We might call this play—which in fact is a fantasy or at least is based on a fantasy process—a myth. It is a story or stories that we have developed or absorbed to explain how we have gotten where we are. Only we don't just explain what has already happened and why—we develop a script for what will happen. As we change the story by adjusting our inner hopes and expectations to the external events and happenings of our lives, our myth becomes most importantly an explanation for what we are and what we will become.

But what does all this talk about fantasy and myth have to do with parenthood? We may even feel that this is the area of our life least likely to bend to our wishes or fantasies. But actually, parenthood is the area in which we most consistently and vigorously work at casting our roles. To what other parts in our lives do we look forward with more certainty as children than to our roles as Mommy and Daddy—the models that those closest to us, our parents, have provided us. We may not have seen Dad or Mom in his or her career life, but it is almost a certainty that we acted out our junior versions of their parental activity again and again in our play. We made sense of the adult world and adult behavior through the creation of new and ever more sophisticated Mom and Dad scenarios. Parents are often horrified to hear versions of their own behavior replayed in their children's fantasies. The rewrite is never the same as the original; it is an adapting of the original to make sense of life and our own emotions and needs as a child.

The parts of Mommy and Daddy are, of course, shaped by what we take in from many sources: other adults, TV, and movie heroes. But one of the most potent roles in our play is the one we cast, starting in childhood, for *our child*. Just as the child playing house is weaving the myth that will condition the shape and size of his parent role later on, his early activity, and especially his needs and feelings about himself, will also condition the hopes that he, as an adult, has for his child. Naturally, the hopes and fears we have for our unborn children change as we grow and mature, but it is important to remember—as we play with our idea of our myth—that our children, if we decide to have them, are major characters in our scenarios and that the roles we expect them to play are at least partly shaped before they even appear on the scene.

All of this can seem quite deterministic. I don't have rigid expectations for my children, you might say, or for my husband, or even for what my life must be. I am more like the audience who responds to life with either appreciation or disappointment, who takes the characters in the play, be they children or adults, for what they are. That is an easier view of ourselves to *accept*, but it often does not allow us full awareness as parents. So it is the *active* authorship of scripts and events that we wish to focus on here.

One of the reasons this responsibility is harder to accept is that for the most part the scenarios we write and rewrite for ourselves and others are unconscious. We become aware of them only when something disrupts the play or someone sees us or a child in a role that we had never imagined or designed for ourselves. We may feel bewildered when an active child demands limits and discipline from us because we had pictured ourselves fitting more comfortably into a laissez-faire role. Many parents question the type of parent they have been when they must face, for example, the case of a child with newly discovered learning disabilities. It is at those times that we can become aware that what we see and expect in ourselves and in our children is conditioned by what we have wanted and needed to see. And the things we have missed are parts of our play or of ourselves that we have purposely left out.

It is also precisely because our scenarios are for the most part unconscious that they have such power over our perceptions and expectations. If we *know* we have a bad temper, we can learn to control it by counting to thirty-five or kicking the wall or whatever. But if we have cast ourselves in a role that does not allow the expression of any anger and we have not given our character any knowledge of how to deal with it, the temper may very well start to control us. Anything that is vague or undefined, whether inside or outside ourselves, is harder to get a handle on—or understand. The things we don't understand always seem like intrusions in our life, even when they come from inside ourselves.

It is because we don't know our own scenarios that they are so powerful. And the reason understanding our myths and fantasies about parenthood has been chosen as the first task in this book is because as parents we have the ability and even the responsibility to assign roles to people who have not yet acquired enough identity of their own to know if they want to play them. Perhaps now you can see the dilemma. It is impossible for us not to assign our children roles. We have to have some vision of what they can become. But at the same time the roles we cast can keep us from seeing their uniqueness and hinder our ability to help them become what they truly are. Without our myths our lives would in a sense be chaotic, but not becoming aware of the function of these myths can also doom us to a lack of growth and to continually problematic relationships.

The key is understanding. And understanding comes most basically through attention. If we pay attention to our perceptions of others and of ourselves as expressions of our inner wishes and needs, we can allow ourselves and others to grow. If we pay attention to our expectations for our children and others as expressions of our scenarios, we can start to evolve those roles to fit the real people and their needs and identities. But what we usually fail to understand is that the myth is our own. It is the story not so much of our lives as of the growth, as we would like it to happen, of our own identities—the unique stories of who we are and what we want to become. The other roles in our stories, though they may help us to appreciate other people, are descriptions not so much of what they are as of what we want from them—or, in reality, what we want from ourselves. If we want a child who will accomplish great things or who will embody certain traits, most often these are things or traits that we would like to accomplish or possess for ourselves. The more we realize the personalness of our myths—and agree to pay attention to them and *own* them—the more our own identities will expand and the more clearly we will see the needs and traits of those around us.

We can be aware of and claim our own myths, and when we do, the myths themselves will give us the keys to our own needs. They will make our identities more distinct and evolving; they will make our values more obvious (all of which we explore in other chapters); and they will give a power and direction to *our* lives that will help us to begin *becoming* the person whose story we are engaged in writing. At this point we will take a look at some of the common elements in parental myths. For like all myths in all cultures, there are universal plots and character types. The following passage is Harold's myth. This is how he sees his fantasy family.

THE WOMAN ON THE HILL

There is a woman who lives high above a fjord and she is waiting for someone. That someone is me. I give her a child and then go away, but I return at intervals and she is always waiting for me. Finally we have four children, two boys and two two girls—the oldest is a girl. When I go back to visit, we play together in the forests, looking for things hiding in secret places. They ask me questions and I teach them about life. I feel guilty about not being there all the time but the woman and children are content and feel that what I give them is enough and valuable.

The woman wears an apron; she makes pottery and is happy in her role. The place where they live is beautiful but on the edge of danger and I protect them and keep their lives safe.

The backdrop—what is parenting really like?

Harold's myth is an example of a fantasy—not one that contains specific goals and concrete activities, but one that plays with an individual man's imagery of family life and his role. If he were considering marriage now, or parenthood, he would probably have other, more concrete, scenarios—depending on who his wife-to-be was and the circumstances of their lives. But this myth of "The Woman on the Hill" contains the essence of his ideal—a script that is obviously not meant for real people but one that fulfills an ideal image that he has of life and of himself. His inner drama contains certain universal themes that give pictures of needs this man might have in a family situation, and even ways he might cast his role.

What we expect to get from parenting is often more clearly expressed in such a deliberate fantasy than in our ruminations about what diaper changing, night feedings, or even helping with homework might be like. The far-out fantasy says more about our psychic-emotional needs; the concrete fantasy helps prepare us for the reality of our roles.

In this story the most obvious thing is that the man is not always there but comes and goes, leaving the job of giving actual physical and emotional sustenance to the woman. He sees the children as a gift he gives her but in his intermittent visiting sees himself no less important than she to the children's lives. It is evident that parenthood is not his whole life—it does not demand more of his psychic or physical energy than he allows it to—and yet it gives his life importance in the ways that he allows it to—and deems it should.

Parenthood actually seems a respite from his real activities—its scene is removed from the world and from Harold's usual sphere of activity and is set in a scene that is restful, quiet, and renewing. His woman is content, rooted to the earth in her pottery making, and she is a complement to his roving, adventuring self. The children are extensions of his curious self and as such give credence to his role as teacher, understander, and interpreter of life; as extensions of himself, they comprise a harmonious whole. But the essence of all the characters is their appreciation and validation of his own identity. They enhance his sense of self by accepting him as he is and seeing him as important and integral to their well-being.

One mistake we might make in looking at this myth, or any other, is that of judging its content or thinking that it applies literally to reality. Were this man married, he

probably would not expect his wife actually to live sep-
arately, raise their children by herself, or spend her time
making pottery. Her rootedness and stability are as important to *his* identity, however, as his adventuring is—
and if he saw his actual partner as having to embody those
qualities expressed in his myth, her own identity (even
if rooted and stable) would be in danger of being ob-
scured. If he could see these as internal needs that could
be met in a family situation, then he could structure his
own role to meet those needs in himself.

Perhaps the important aspects to note in looking at how
his myth might affect the reality of Harold's own family
life are (1) his need to be appreciated in his role; (2) his
ability to define the extent and nature of his involvement;
(3) his success in the identity he has set up for himself
as a parent, teacher, interpreter of life, and protector; and
(4) his perception of parenthood as a place of respite
from the tensions of his other roles and as a source of renewal and refreshment.

These four images are common ideals we have for parenthood, both as mothers and as fathers, both before and
after we become parents. But these images make us particularly vulnerable to the realities of parenthood, either
because we have not examined our expectations or because we haven't developed a realistic view before becoming parents, of what the demands of parenthood are like.

Awareness of our inner needs and of how they express
themselves in terms of our expectations is a powerful tool
that can help us to prevent or deal with some of the frustration and disappointment that occur when these inner
needs are not met. When we make decisions about becoming a parent or examine our dissatisfactions with or confusion about our roles, we can benefit from looking at our
fantasy pictures—not just the current ones, but old ones
too. The process itself can be relaxing and fun. And instead
of judging those pictures on the basis of reality, look at

the needs they express—for solitude, renewal, affirmation, identity—and at the way fantasy and reality can work together to make our lives more whole.

Myths give us clues to what we expect from our lives at a particular time and the way we hope our lives will mesh with our personal needs. To become more aware of our expectations for behavior—both our own and others—we have to look at our cast of characters. Those mythical figures can have a definitive effect on both our relationships and the way we choose to pursue our roles.

The cast of characters

I. The ideal parent

Obviously, most of the modeling we have for parenting has come from our own parents. But our ideals will also come from what was lacking in our parents and what we wanted our parents to be. Our inner fantasy of the parent we will become, or should be, is expressed in our expectations for ourselves and, if we are parents already, in our feelings about our own behavior.

Who did we feel we would be? We might get in touch with this first by asking ourselves who, in addition to our own parents, we had for parent models during our childhood and youth. Did we have models from books, movies, TV, of how a parent should act or feel? What capacities or traits did we value in our own parents and what did we find missing? What did we feel our parents could be?

Dr. E. Pecci, a psychiatrist in private practice in California, has an interesting technique for getting in touch with the ideal parent within us. He suggests closing our eyes and imagining we are adolescents again. In that regressed state he asks us then to imagine our parents as we saw them through our adolescent eyes. When we get a picture of our parents then, we are to imagine what we saw they could be and to get in touch with our feelings about the discrepancy between their potential and what they actually were as we saw them. He suggests doing this by fantasizing about our same-sex parent. We can then translate this into some of the powerful ideals we have for ourselves.[1]

For some of us this exercise might be painful. The disparity between what we know someone wants or feels they could be and what they are can be disturbing. But our ability to locate our own feelings about this can help us in at least two ways. It can help us to see the kinds of expectations, reasonable or unreasonable, that we bring to parenting. These can help us to grow or doom us to failure before we even start. And we can learn some important lessons about ourselves and who we think we are.

Our ideals will often furnish us with what psychotherapist Phillip Mitchell calls "mistaken certainties." These are some of the beliefs that underlie our everyday behavior. As ideas they may be sound, but Mitchell calls them "mistaken" because once we have adopted them, we tend to use them without evaluating their usefulness for a given situation.[2]

"Mistaken" suggests that the ideas are not wrong, only misused or too extensively applied. Mitchell cites the example of a belief in hard work as a valuable concept, but one that is inappropriate when we are trying to learn to relax.

This example may seem obvious, but the ways that our "shoulds" about "good" parenting affect our identities, our needs, and our behavior are subtle.

> A good parent always puts the child's needs first.
> A good parent is always supportive.
> A good parent treats each child equally and always feels the same toward them.

These are examples of constructive attitudes that have been distorted into certainties. No one would be capable of actually achieving any of these goals, nor would it be desirable. His behavior would become too compulsive and arbitrary.

Perhaps the essential problem is that our ideal makes us believe in the concept of the "good parent," which is fallacious in itself. There are behaviors and attitudes that are basically more constructive in relationships, but if we apply them like Band-Aids to our children's problems they cannot have their intended effect. If we defer to someone else's needs out of a sense of duty, we will most likely only make him feel guilty. He may even take advantage of us. But if we do it out of a genuine desire to meet his needs, both of us benefit. The idea of the "good parent" in the abstract often merely keeps us from growing. Our ideal can help us sort out the qualities in ourselves that we prize, the goals we want to move toward. This is one way we can check up on our ideal parents to see if they are serving us well. Do they help us to be more discriminating in knowing how to handle situations? Or do they hand us "shoulds" that make us confused or rigid in our reactions?

Our ideal parents are tricky. We need to be aware of them and respect them in order to put our most constructive energy into parenthood. We also have to let them evolve. If our ideal parents do not change with our experience, they are not meeting our needs for growth. If we cling to our ideals too tenaciously, they will limit our understanding of ourselves and our children. They may make us prescribe behavior for our spouses and other people around us. Our ideal parents belong to us. They should not, if they are helping us, furnish us with goals for others. We need to pay attention to our ideals, but if we focus on them too exclusively it will be hard for us to see the effects of that other major character:

II. The shadow parent: can we admit his existence?

Just as our image of the ideal parent both inspires our behavior and constantly reminds us where we or others are
falling short, there is perhaps another person inside us all
whose presence we are not so happy to admit. In simple
terms, we might describe this character as the parent we
are afraid of becoming—the mother or father we never
wanted to be. Most commonly we externalize this parent
—we project him or her onto other people in our cast,
typically our own parents or people we observe with their
children. It's as if the more we see him in others the less
likely it is that he will have any relation to us.

But as parents we are chagrined to find that at certain,
almost predictable, times that shadow parent appears and
wreaks havoc on our self-image and esteem.

One mother who is working on curbing her impulse toward angry outbursts with her children describes her
shadow parent:

He's ferocious, absolutely untouchable by reason. I would
even say he has a desire for revenge when pushed too far. He
comes out when my unsympathetic feelings toward myself go
up and I am in the grips of my ideal: I should be self-sacrific-
ing, I say, willing to give up all my desires for my child's needs,
and then in the midst of expecting too much of myself I let the
children go too far and something snaps inside me—my shadow
parent comes out.

He used to be only a slight tendency when I had one child,
but with the stress of additional children he has become a
whole personality. I used to think the problem was outside me,
that my kids pushed me too far. I am starting to own that
shadow parent as part of me. When I first saw that this was a
problem, I thought I was a terrible person. Now I see myself as
a good person with a problem.

And in trying to work on the problem a new character has
emerged. I call him the inhibitor. He is like a tiny voice in the
nethermost region of my brain. I picture him as a tiny man

about a half-inch tall jumping up and down in a cavern shouting, "Don't do that," when I'm about to hit my kids.

Someday I picture he will become a part of me. My shadow will become very feeble and my ideal more human. I think the key will be my becoming a person who can recognize, explain, and take care of my own needs.

At first we are shocked: "Before I had a child I vowed I would never act some of the ways that I saw other parents acting. But now sometimes I act just the ways I never thought I would." Why? Perhaps it is because we didn't understand the trials and tribulations of parenthood, and now that we do, it makes ultimate sense to act that way sometimes. But it is also just as valid to say that these reactions were existing inside us, waiting to make their entrance on certain cues in the parenting role.

How big this shadow parent gets will depend on at least three *interrelating* factors. (1) our understanding of how he appears, his presence, what he's like, what touches him off—brings him out, as it were—will depend on the kind of childhood we had and the negative schemas we absorbed from our own parent figures; (2) our awareness and understanding of how he reacts, when he is liable to step forth, will help us determine what reactions we can substitute in his place; (3) our ability and our feelings about doing the latter will also depend on whether or not our own needs are being met. If we are not having our needs for love, financial security, growth, social or intellectual stimulation, or self-esteem met, it is easy for this shadow parent to make us feel that his appearance is beyond our control.

What we have to do to begin is to have the courage to meet him face-to-face. Just as with the ideal parent, we may find that parts of him are laughable or just plain obsolete—that we have grown beyond those qualities or that only our fear of them and our denial of them have kept them hanging around. We may be horrified to find that

he looks just like our mother or father. We may be happy
to find that perhaps we have judged him wrongly and
parts of him are not so bad and in certain situations perfectly appropriate. When we meet him we will discover
that we can control his behavior by paying attention to
him, by acknowledging his existence rather than denying it.

Somewhere in between the ideal and shadow is the real
person who exists in spite of all our preconceived images
and scripts for our behavior. If we can move toward the
idea that *what we are* will affect our children more than
the techniques we use on them or even what we do, our
idea of ourselves as parents can grow. We can get in
touch then with the true responsibility of *being* and becoming a parent—the responsibility for our own growth.

Dr. Richard Farson commented in one interview:

We have treated our children as if we could shape them the
way a sculptor shapes clay . . . but that's not the way it is. It's
more like we are running along and we fall on a pile of clay;
we leave an impression all right, and that impression is dis-
tinctly us, but we have very little control of what it looks like.

You see, in child raising what parents are is terribly important. I suspect that kindness and decency, for instance, are
learned by being around mothers and fathers who are kind
and decent, and the same is true of other qualities. Parents who
have high aspirations for themselves seem to produce children
who have high aspirations. Hypochondriacs tend to produce
hypochondriacs. Obviously, children learn a lot from us, though
it's not always what we want them to learn.[3]

Becoming aware of our *scripts for ourselves* can increase
our acceptance and knowledge of who we are. It can open
new options for changing our attitudes and behavior.
However, seeing ourselves also paves the way for seeing
the people around us more clearly. Having examined what
we expect from ourselves as parents, it follows that we will

begin to see the qualities we have ascribed to that other major character in our myth—the child.

III. The child: how does he fit into the cast?

As one woman described the immediate shift from expectations to reality:

> I was sure my baby would be a boy. We had talked about a girl's name for maybe a few minutes all those months but spent endless time discussing boys' names. Our child was going to be a big, muscular boy like my husband. I had no picture of myself as a mother, but of what my husband's kid was going to look like. I wasn't in there at all . . . I wasn't disappointed when Emily was born. I adored her from the start.

To think that we see a newborn or even a growing child for what he is, is to deny our humanness. In every culture the idea of giving birth to a child has deep psychic significance, centering around the idea of bringing forth new hope, perfection, and potential for the race. All cultures have archetypal images of giving birth to the "divine child" who will bring new life to humanity. The strong imagery we have about our children may be the most difficult for us to recognize or sort out. The idea of having expectations for parenthood and for ourselves seems only natural, as we tend to anticipate all our life changes and try them out in fantasy. However, if you ask an expectant couple what they want in their unborn child, they will most often insist vehemently that *all* they want is a healthy baby. To articulate more seems to be tempting fate. And yet, especially during pregnancy, mothers report themselves as being flooded with fantasies and dreams about the baby still forming inside them. The fantasies are not about the developing fetus but about a baby, often in their own image, with distinguishable sex, personality, and, perhaps most important, reactions to their mothers. During what other time in our lives do we have a longer or more intense buildup for meeting someone—not to mention our long-term investment in what he will be like? It is not surprising, then, that people can be frightened or superstitious about these fantasies. They are apt to contain images that can be unaccountably unpleasant or fulfilling. Most prenatal instructors do not encourage parents to discuss their fantasies, but those educators who have report the understandings that result as being beneficial even in a long-range sense.

Some people try to limit the extent of their involvement in the pregnancy experience, including its strange feelings and fantasies, because they are afraid of psychological damage. There is little rationale for these feelings; severe emotional problems during pregnancy are rare. There is even evidence that those individuals who are most fully conscious of the changes of pregnancy have the least trouble for making the necessary adjustment after the baby is born.[4]

Psychologist Gerald Caplan sees the expression of prenatal fantasies in a sympathetic environment as good preventive psychiatry and feels that a woman who is *absorbed* in certain fears or indicates certain problems in relation to the coming child and receives counseling at that time can avoid a distortion in the relationship with her child.[5]

One young woman had postponed any fantasy image of a baby she might have because of her experiences with her baby sister, who was diagnosed at an early age as autistic. After taking a live-in job as a baby-sitter for a family with a new baby, she realized that her image of her own fantasy child could safely emerge. Shortly after moving in, she made this journal entry:

7-12 I was thinking about having a child the other night. I was thinking that I wasn't afraid of a baby anymore because of Marie. Always before the thought of having a child would make me feel miserable. . . . It was like my sister blocked out my ability to even imagine having a child. I think I was afraid the whole cycle would begin again. I was afraid that my fantasy child would just be there and not move. In a sense I had a baby that wasn't real but that was always damaged. But now with Marie, she's so bright and happy—so much more, people say, than even most babies. She is strong physically and beautiful in the way she moves. My sister rarely talked if ever. But Marie talks even now at 3 months. She talks all the time and it makes me so happy to see her. What surprises me now is my own eagerness to put this happy experience in my mind instead of the unhappy one. Perhaps it was knowing Marie from birth. . . . I guess good experiences don't automatically wipe out the bad ones. But if one is willing I am amazed at how efficiently they do.

IV. Relating to the ideal child

Most of us have an unconscious image of an ideal child, a child who will be everything we want him to be, who will even look a certain way (the physical images are sometimes quite specific), and who responds to us in ways that make us feel self-satisfied and more complete. Our image is actually a description of our own potential—things we would like to complete in ourselves. When our real child is born, we probably at least compare him with our ideal—parents often find their real child far more wonderful than any fantasy—however, if he is obviously very different, we can mourn the child we had created in our imaginations and grown to know.

Therapists who work with families who have given birth to a disabled infant make two assumptions: the infant is a complete distortion of the dreamed-of or planned-for infant, and the parents must mourn the loss of this imagined infant before they can become attached to the living defective one.[6]

William Kotzwinkle's moving story relates not only the vitality of that ideal child in our psychic life, but the power of fantasy to create and extend our emotional lives, to integrate our losses and riches both now and in the past. The author describes a father driving home from the hospital following the stillbirth of his first son:

And then he saw himself running with his son through the fields, leaping the old broken fences. They walked to the stream and dived into it, then danced upon it, then ran to the trees, climbing up above the mist.

Laski drove toward home with tears streaming down his face, his spirit racing with his son through time, across the morning of the world, in cities and in the lovely valley. The moment of their meeting was endless. They took a boat and took a train and saw the sights and grew up together.

He's going now, thought Laski. He's growing up and leaving me. Good-by, good-by, he called, looking out to the beautiful eastern sky where the sun was dazzling the trees.[7]

Giving birth to someone who at first fits and maintains our ideal can also be challenging. Sometimes we fall in love with our baby as the image of our "ideal child" and then become disappointed, as we will point out later, as she starts to show a personality of her own. As one woman said:

It took me three years to be comfortable about being a mother. Now it's starting to be fun. Although the first months were physically exhausting there was, nevertheless, a honeymoon quality of excitement and a novelty about them. But that ended when the baby began to sit up, to toddle, to show temper, to make terrifyingly clear to a mother that this was a person for whose emotional development she was responsible. This challenge . . . seemed to catalyze her own inner flaws—immaturity, dependence, confusion about her role.[8]

Although none of us runs precisely the same course in our development as parents or carries with us the identical box full of fantasies, there are certain periods that predictably evoke these personal myths and pictures. At these crucial points we are forced to choose between the inner and outer realities, or at least to adjust to them. There are common stages of parental development. We have already considered the anticipatory images that precede the child's birth. Other important phases can be grouped as follows:

1. After birth when there is an inevitable adjustment to some tangible aspects of the new reality. If we have a boy, we can no longer hold onto our picture of this baby as a girl. If the baby resembles our father, we have to let go of an image we had of a different-looking child.

During this period, much of the testing of our fantasy life and adjustment to reality has to do with our discoveries of our strengths and enjoyments as well as our inadequacies in fitting into our roles as we had previously scripted them. This is especially true for the mother, as we shall see in the chapter on identity. The father's test for the performance of his role can start much later, be more compartmentalized; but a woman's test of her inner images of motherhood begins way before birth—even before she has decided to have a child.

There is also an initial and often traumatic adjustment at this time between fantasies about the tasks of parenthood and the actual demands. The shock seems to have less to do with the parent's ability to adjust to and meet the daily demands of her new baby than with the potency of her individual myth and how flexible it proves.

2. The toddler. When a child hits eighteen months or thereabouts, her growth often leads us into the next big readjustment. Tension results from the assertions of her own identity and her simultaneous demands for limits and directives which give her clues to her own role in her expanding world.

This stage, when the toddler's typical response to everything is "No," often symbolizes more than a simple rejection of our immediate demands. This resistance forces us to give up many of our baby images and infancy roles for our child: the complete dependency, the passive self waiting to be molded, the acceptor of all our love and affection.

For many parents this new independence and shift in relationship may signal relief, especially if their scenario had not depicted infancy as the most important scene. But for many parents the stage of infancy is hard to give up, and our enjoyment of that stage may encourage us to bring in a new actor to fill the vacant role—in the form of a new baby.

This period also gives us an opportunity to expand our roles and give up or modify some of the early images we held of ourselves as parents. We must at least closely examine the validity of our stereotypes of ourselves as, for example, the Nurturer, the All-giving Parent Who Never Says No, the Shaper and Supplier of Reality.

3. Having our second, third, fourth, or fifth child causes a reevaluation of our scenarios for all family members including ourselves. The cast changes—our baby can become an older sibling or a middle child overnight. Not only will we look at our children differently, but their conceptions of their roles will be changed. It is up to us to help them integrate their perceptions of their new roles.

This reassessment does not just occur at the birth of the new baby as we commonly assume. Each time someone in the family changes—the baby becomes a walker or goes to school, the oldest becomes a teenager, or the mother or father changes careers or interests—everyone in the family has to reexamine who he is in relation to everyone else in the family.

4. The next adjustment commonly comes whenever we send our child to school.

Our child's adjustment to and performance in school, whether at the age of two or at another age, brings in another view of reality to test our inner images. That reality is what our child's teachers give us in the form of their perceptions of our children and of us. Often we must give up our images and hopes for our child—as class genius, as the most popular, the most generous child. And our images of ourselves as supercompetent parent, our child's protector from hurt, may be threatened by any negative feedback from school staff. If a father sees his image of himself as linked to his child's achievement, then his child's actual school performance may cause him to test his own performance in his fantasies for himself as father.

5. Adolescence. Through the teenager's assertion of his own identity we become aware that much of our original scenario for that child may never happen. In this situation we may also find ourselves fearful that some negative scenes that we have been trying to suppress ultimately may be played out. Our handling of this stage may hinge on how we have handled our fantasy images in other stages of his and our development. If we have become increasingly aware of how our hopes and fears for our children are actually tied up with hopes and fears we have for ourselves, then we will be able to view our children more and more as their own emerging selves.

So creating our own myth or scenario, periodically revising it, and even giving up crucial parts of it are as integral to the parenting process as they are to our own growth.

Myths mistaken for reality

We tend to label our children's personality traits. From early infancy we view our babies and define our children's personalities by "people we see in them." This is probably one of the important ways we have of dealing with our anxieties about the unknown. Seeing familiar traits and looks in our babies and our children can make the task of raising them seem a trifle easier. However, the danger is that we are only recognizing these aspects of our children because they are part of the scenario we have written for them. Unless we are aware of what it is, both in ourselves and in them, that causes us to characterize them that way, we can never be sure if we are stifling or encouraging their development.

It is true that our children often look strikingly like us or someone we know, and depending on our relationship with this person or our feelings about ourselves, the resemblance can affect our feelings toward our child markedly. We can also see personality characteristics in them that remind us of others. The most distressing comparisons we make concern traits we see in them that we dislike in ourselves. An abused child in a family is frequently the one child who has traits such as temper or moodiness, or an appearance that has unpleasant associations for a parent. Being aware of those associations can help to free our perceptions of the child and allow us to see his individuality.

Recognition is probably one of the most important processes for us to be aware of in our relationships with our children. Through our awareness of what we are seeing in them, based on our own associations and previous experience, we can begin to sort out their actual personality traits and approaches to their experience. This understanding of a child's individual nature comes through examining our own wishes and fears for him. It can be helped by observation of him as well as by knowledge of other children and their behavior at the same stage. Our inability to see through what we "project" onto children —like slides onto a screen—can be the biggest hindrance to meeting their needs for healthy growth and development. We all engage in this projecting process to some degree. Those who can become actively aware of it will have the greatest chance of nurturing those seeds of individual potential that reside in every child and guiding behavior according to realistic expectations.

Much of what we do as parents requires little analysis and introspection. We may be satisfied and even proud of the way we handle things. Many people find their self-esteem benefited by parenting in ways for which their expectations never prepared them. Awareness is a tool we can use at times, especially in transitions, in order to stretch our abilities to deal with complicated situations and demands. This does not mean a perpetual analysis of our children or ourselves. Nothing could make parenthood more boring or tedious.

Insight into our personal myths can benefit us throughout our life. However, there are certain periods when an understanding of our myths and fantasies is especially useful in offering us guidance. When we or our children are undergoing basic life change when we start to see each other in new ways, the imagery of our inner vision may be indispensable in preparing us for the new realms we're entering. The prime example of this sort of transition is the time that we spend preparing our inner and outer lives for the birth of our child, as we will discuss in the next chapter.

Interviews

Looking at our pictures of parenting:
before and after

Our pictures of what parenthood would be like can be quite vivid. Looking at these pictures helps us to uncover our hidden expectations for ourselves and our family.

Joan, age 32; two children, ages 4, 1½:

I aways knew I would be a mother. It was a given . . . it was a question of when. I didn't feel any professional conflict. I'd worked a bit, I'd accomplished something. School was over. It was time to embark, but it wasn't a clear decision.

I always had a picture of a mother as a woman in the kitchen, doing for my kids; a feeling of creativeness, singing songs, getting into play—a light side of myself. I was excited to have a baby, watch it grow, have it evolve. I would be a follower, not a leader of my children. I would have a spunky, active, curious child.

Patti, age 28; child, age 5:

I wanted something to love and to love me back. I liked the idea of a family, a kind of a unit—a mother, father, and two or three kids. I like kids and the things you do with kids. I like hiking, tennis, bike riding, physical things. I liked to see the developing times—to see them do different things, help them grow, communicate with them, hear ideas . . .

Mica, age 35; three children, ages 8, 6, 7 months:

I loved being around children so much that I couldn't wait to have one of my own. But it was so different from just playing with someone else's child. I loved him (still do) so intensely that everything he did was of the utmost fascination. I was surprised that my friends couldn't see how absolutely fascinating he was (they thought he was cute like all babies). When I was pregnant with the second I was afraid I could never love another child as much as I had the first. But I was just as overwhelmed by her, and with the third the very special part is having the older children who become just as excited by everything she does as I do.

Rick, age 33; two children, ages 6, 4:

Before parenthood I had the image of having boys I could go hiking with who would like the same things I liked. Outdoors kind of people. Girls too. I imagined spending a lot of time teaching the children things and showing them things, taking them on trips and sharing the exploration and wonder with them.

It turned out that I found instead an outlet for my heart and affection. What impressed me was that while I was anticipating a lot of shared activities, the real emphasis has been on shared emotions and love.

Sandy, age 30; two children, ages 3, 18 months:

I always assumed I would be a mother. It was one of the things that came with being married. It was just a question of waiting for the best time, partly waiting for the right housing—which was somewhat difficult in London—and then I was getting on to thirty. I felt if I had my children before I was thirty, I would be able to get back into a job by around thirty or so. I was doing some research for my master's thesis and I figured I would be finished before my first child was born.

Mary, age 28; two children, ages 5, 2:

I decided to have children because I wanted to have more people to love. I didn't even think about having children before I got married. I pictured that my days would have a pattern; I envisioned myself rising at eight, feeding and dressing the baby, putting her down, feeding her at noon, putting her down—a regular routine.

The way it was, was not at all the same because I had to consider people around me. I was breast-feeding. My parents lived near us and were uncomfortable about my nursing Emily in front of them. I had to remove myself. I would have to get her up when she was sleeping to show her off to relatives, or dress her up to show her off. Emily was a good baby, very tiny, a small eater who ate often, a happy baby, but kind of nervous. She seemed to startle easily, was very responsive to stimuli.

As author Angela McBride states so succinctly:

If you remember being loved by your parents, you probably want to have a child to find out what it feels like to be admired the way you admired your own parents. I think this is more likely than because you are dying to give love. Having a child may mean that you are finally emancipated from your own parents. Once I was pregnant, I expected them to see me as an equal, mature, no more their "flighty kid." Having a baby is a rite of transition. For a woman to be considered fully "grown-up" in much of American society, she has to have children. If she wants people to listen to her as a responsible person, she has to be able to show her credentials—Tom, Ann, Billy, Wendy, and so forth.

I even remember looking forward to the time when I could complain and say, "That child is always on the go; I *always* have to be right behind her or she'll get in trouble; it's a wonder I'm not bone thin." I grew up hearing variations on this theme and I wanted an excuse to complain back . . . I wanted some of the sympathy society reserves for mothers.[9]

Miriam, age 33; child, age 1:

One of the things I fantasized about before was the affection. . . . But we were so taken aback by the intensity of our love for him. Some friends came over when Benjamin was about four months old, two friends without children. I mentioned that I had never loved anyone as much before. Benjamin's father was in the next room, and they said "Shh." They thought it would ruin our relationship for him to hear that. And I laughed and said, "But he feels exactly the same way."

Just now he's learning to hug and it has such a powerful effect on me. I just melt. It makes my day.

I'm astounded at how having a baby has changed my feeling toward my own mother. It's something that's hard to verbalize but I just appreciate her so much more.

Mary, age 56; three children, ages 35, 28, 26:

I never thought about exactly what it would be like to have children, but after I had them it was so rewarding. We were so poor and they were sick a lot but those hardships didn't matter because we had the children. It made us want to better ourselves, to have a better house, to learn more. Anything we did we did for the children. They gave us our meaning in life. Before you have children you're alone, but I feel now that for the rest of my life I won't be alone because parts of me have grown out in all these separate ways. They will always be the most important people to me.

Q.: What was your picture of what it would be like
to be a mother?

A.: My picture of motherhood was worse than it
turned out. I had this picture of a harassed mother
with a squalling, dirty baby. The reality has been
more pleasant. I wonder why *other* parents don't get
as much joy.

Janet, age 17:

I always thought of having a baby, not of having a
child. I always pictured K. as a baby, not as an eight-
year-old.

Gail, age 37; two children, ages 6, 4:

Q.: Why did you decide to have children?

A.: I never decided. I was programmed to do it. I
was really very anxious about it. I was thirty years
old when I first became pregnant. I felt it was something I should do and needed to get done.

Q.: Did you have a picture of what it would be like
to be a parent, a mother?

A.: Part of my picture was a fantasy. We'd walk to
the library, read stories, listen to records—and a lot of
that came true with my first child.

Diane, age 35; two children, ages 12, 9:

I wasn't interested in children before I had my own.
I had them when I did because my husband wanted
to. But after they were born I thought they were
the greatest. We had gone over to a friend's house
when I was pregnant the first time. He was an artist
(I am too) and he had kids. We asked him what it
was like. He said they think and say the greatest
things. That made me feel so good when I was
pregnant.

The most wonderful thing is seeing them grow. It's a privilege to see the changes. The most amazing first change is watching the humanity and reason emerge in them. It's wonderful to see them able to communicate with reason. I loved watching my daughter when she first realized she was pretty, when my children started taking pride in their accomplishments, when they wanted to do it all by themselves. My daughter just wrote a poem about the joy and sadness of Christmas and it's beautiful seeing the poetry awaken in them.

Susan, age 33; two children, ages 6, 4:

After birth—the radiance, the glowingness of the child, so bright that it seems for days I literally can't take my eyes off him. I can't sleep. I am too high. I lie for hours staring at him. I feel giddy. I look from him to our surroundings—to the world outside his window and everything, everything seems infused with this mad radiance and underlying meaning and love.

Carol, age 31; three children, ages 4, 3, 1:

Jamie's birth separated Jim and me physically for the first time. He wasn't a girl—he was loud, ugly, and demanding from the start. I realized then we weren't talking about a doll, but a child. I thought Jamie would change and (our life-style was great) adjust to us. Even the nurse in the hospital told me he was a very demanding baby, with real temper tantrums even as a tiny infant. A "good baby" for me would be one who slept all night long, who would thrive.

Edith:

I had very little experience with children under three, but I thought I was terribly experienced (I had

worked in preschools and grade schools). I had everything to learn about babies. I was worried that I
couldn't communicate with babies. I was concerned
about the birth process. I wanted to have a beautiful
birth, no pain. I wanted to breast-feed. I wanted perfect children, physically, emotionally, mentally. I
never thought I would have any difficulty. I would
have very agreeable infants—and I did. So I guess in
that sense my expectations were met.

Alta:

I had a baby to see if I really could do it, to see if I
could make a baby. I had a picture of being a mother
like a stained-glass window. I assumed it would be a
boy, a happy threesome, that he would look like his
dad.

Dick, age 33; two children, ages 6, 4:

There was something unsubstantial about our home
life. It felt like children could in some way anchor us.
When the kids came it felt like we were precipitated
into a structured world we had never come to terms
with before. My urge to assume structure was really
an urge toward greater maturity. I wanted a more
mature attitude toward responsibility, career, et
cetera. I had always had a problem relating to adult
responsibilities. Children successfully and very satis-
fyingly drew me a little further on in my growth. As
much as it was a conflict between my habitual styles
and the new needs of the family, my aspiration was
tied to the future and in a sense the family guided
me through that transition.

Shedding our expectations

Letting go of what we thought we would be as parents and what we thought our children would be like can help us feel more effective. This parent shares some of her fantasies and the ways she worked on seeing through them. during her first year as a mother.

Rachel, age 30; two children, ages 6, 3:

Prior to the birth of my first child I had lost three babies through early miscarriage and then went through a tense two-year period when I was unable to conceive. Having a baby became an overwhelming desire and goal for me from the beginning of our marriage. Even though I was only in my early twenties and still a college undergraduate with fuzzy career aims, I had believed strongly that this was the ideal time to have a child. I thought that starting our family when we were young, energetic, and not rigidly set into a life-style would be the best idea. And in this fantasy, which for me then seemed a real possibility, our baby would fit so easily into my life that I would be able to finish my schooling, even up past graduate school, or get a full-time job even when the baby was an infant, without counting on child care or equal assistance from my husband.

I pictured a calm, happy, alert baby (who in my fantasy was born with the physical characteristics of a six-month-old Gerber advertisement) who ate at regular intervals and slept most of the rest of the time. Or who would be able to entertain himself when awake by playing with his hands, watching light patterns on the wall, or admiring a colorful crib mobile.

Jacob's birth, though almost a month premature, was perfect: astonishingly fast—only a little more than two hours of labor—and almost painless. I had been apprehensive about the birth process. Since I am small I almost assumed I couldn't deliver the baby in the normal way, or at very least I would need quite a lot of medication during my labor and delivery. I was, throughout my pregnancy, far more concerned about the brief labor and delivery stage of parenthood than preparing for the day-to-day reality of life with a baby. For example, I dropped out of the Red Cross mother and infant care class after only two sessions in order to attend my Lamaze childbirth class religiously.

The birth was so precipitous, so easy. I was numb. I felt even in those first elated hours after Jacob's birth that he had come too fast and too soon. I wasn't ready to have a baby. And what happened with him in his early months, the type of baby he was and the child he became, differed vastly from my fantasy.

He slept most of the time the first week when I was staying with my mother. Most of that time I felt giddily confident, even a little guiltily bored. He nursed well and then went right to sleep. I couldn't even show him off. The only inkling I got that week of the later sense of being ill-prepared for the tasks and incompetent for the role was that I couldn't diaper him fast enough to please myself. I struggled with the pins so long that he sometimes messed himself again while I was still diapering.

Once I brought him home, this changed suddenly. He woke up. I would nurse him, try to burp him with no success, call the pediatric nurse who assured me that breast-fed babies didn't burp after feeding, and then attempt to put him down. Immediately he would start howling and turn red in the face—with what I interpreted as being indignant rage. I would pick him up, nurse him back to sleep, and rock him for what seemed like hours. Within forty-five minutes after I would finally get him in his crib, he would be up and screaming again. The only time it seemed he was quiet or relaxed at all was when he was nursing. The rest of the time he was fretful. Even his sleep was a thrashing, disturbed kind of rest.

I called my mother several times. She suggested that he was not getting enough to eat. She had bottle-fed all her children and was skeptical from the start that I would be able to nourish my son on mother's milk alone. I called the pediatrician, who said that I could try giving him a bottle every third feeding. I was mortified and felt completely defeated. My baby was less than a month old, and already I was unable to do what other mothers could do with no trouble. But I would do anything to make that baby stop crying. I gave him the bottle—in which he showed little interest—and then an hour later he was turning purple and squirming.

Something in me made me stick with the nursing and give up on the idea of forcing him to drink formula from a bottle. I just didn't believe that his feeding needs were the problem.

So, even by the end of the first month—a milestone at which point many child development experts assured me in baby magazines and paperbacks that I would be on top of things with my child and tuned into his every need—I was completely floored. I was constantly tearful and floundering about with a baby whose cues I could not seem to read, despite my pre-natal classes, despite the well-meaning advice of parents and sisters-in-law, and certainly despite the often contradictory counsel of Spock, Dodson, Gesell, et al.

I was, I cried, saddled with an infant who did not, as Spock assured me he would, sleep almost twenty hours a day in the early weeks. On the contrary, it was rare for him to sleep more than three hours at a stretch, day or night. He did not fall into a four-, three-, or even two-hour nursing schedule within these early weeks and months. I did not learn, as I was promised I would, by his cry, in some instinctual way, whether he was hungry, thirsty, wet, gassy, or bored. And there were long foggy days when it seemed that all I did was nurse him momentarily into silence or rock him, and that I cried as much as my baby.

I lived in a city at the time in a neighborhood where there were few women of my age who spoke English and/or who had small children. I found other parents through the local public health center discussion group for mothers of infants, and later through the Early Learning Center, a resource center for mothers and children under three. When I say "through," I mean precisely that; out of both groups I formed friendships with women whose life-styles and general ideas about child raising complemented mine. From these women I found my basic supports and occasionally useful, practical advice.

What we all seemed to need was reassurance we were doing OK, that our children, despite colic, diaper rash, and poor feeding habits, were OK, that we were not failing in our roles as mothers in some basic way.

And we compared our babies: how much and when they nursed, what they ate and at what age, when they slept and how long at a stretch. Some of this comparing was distressing to me, mother of a fretful one, a tense one, a slow-developing one. There was a period when seeing other babies who seemed always happier, more alert, easier to read, was more depressing than sitting in our third-floor walk-up alone. I had grown up caring for a lot of babies, seeing a lot of babies, and had never had the kind of difficulty reading and responding to them as I did with my own child. As I struggled with him, I began to question my memory. Perhaps I had not been as competent as I'd remembered; perhaps the children had been fussier. And my husband, frustrated and sleepless too, could not stop himself from saying the terrible words: "I thought you said you knew how to be a mother."

It took many months of relaxing a little—as Jacob began to ease up on his crying and increase his sleep —and looking at these other mothers with their babies, to see more clearly that they too had difficulties sometimes—in their attitudes, handling, or personal frustrations—that I never experienced or worked out on my own. That their babies had traits or problems that my child had escaped. And that, while my son's basic personality was and is more high-strung, moodier, and more easily frustrated than many children's, he did change in time and find outlets for his energy and controls for his frustration.

And something else I discovered a little ways up the road with Jacob was that the very same quality that made him difficult to handle as an infant made him very special as a preschooler. His stubbornness translated into perseverance and concentration, his moodiness into sensitivity and imagination, the inability to screen out annoying stimuli into an ability to experiment with all kinds of activities and experiences.

If I wasn't completely convinced by my own observations of other mothers and babies when my son was an infant, that babies are born with very different personalities, my second child sold me on the idea. It seemed, even in utero, that Melissa was a calmer child. While Jacob had dived and thrashed and hiccupped, Melissa placidly thumped. From the moment she was born and placed in my arms, it was clear to me that her body was more relaxed, her disposition evener. I was waiting anxiously the first three weeks for her to wake up and start the same fretful course her brother had followed. She had one or two bad days during her third week, and I almost panicked. I was afraid I couldn't endure again the howling and the constant rocking. But this passed, and she spent her first year or longer in calm observation and sunny play.

The evolving fantasy

Describing our "dream houses" enables us to see our changing pictures of life within our family. As our children become young adults, we may find that our dream has evolved with the actual shifts in our relationships. We may also still be holding on to parts of that original dream that we are not yet ready to give up. As one woman told us:

> The dream that I've envisioned the most often in my life has been a house full of children. I've always wanted to be a mother with many children to love and care for. God has blessed us with five lovely children of our own and opportunities to help in the raising of several others.
>
> Just recently I've come to realize that it is time to "trade in" the old dream for a new, more realistic one.
>
> When one of our older sons left home recently after a rebellious incident with his dad, although I understood the situation intellectually, I was shattered emotionally. My husband described my reaction as similar to a person experiencing the grief of mourning.
>
> With an oldest child of nineteen years, I properly should have prepared myself for the eventuality of

the young leaving the nest. Instead I made the adjustment the hard way, and too quickly I realized that I
had truly accepted this tremendous change in a college class when the instructor asked us to represent
our "dream house." I began like the old woman in
the shoe and put pictures of babies all over the house.
As I looked at it, I became aware that this wasn't my
dream house anymore, unless it was the perfect solution—there were grandchildren in that shoe. So my
dream has evolved, maintaining some elements but
putting me in a different relationship to them.

Our media families

Our ideal parents and perfect child do not arise out of our
imaginations. They are developed from many role models:
from our parents and other parents we have known, and,
for parents of the television generation, out of the wealth
of images from popular TV shows.

Carolyn, mid-30s; three children:
I guess we all have fantasies of child raising. I had
always wanted to have children, and when I did not
have someone to marry by the time I was fifteen, I
thought I was an old maid. Finally, at seventeen, I
became engaged, and I married at nineteen. At last I
could finally try my hand at child rearing. I certainly
had to do a better job than my parents! (I can now
see some of the things my parents did that were quite
good and wish that I had not been so narrow-minded
toward them.)

I didn't want much from the children. I wanted a
boy first and then two girls. The boy was to be like
Beaver in the TV series "Leave It to Beaver," and the
girl was to be like Shirley Temple, and I was to marry

a man as patient and understanding as Robert Young in "Father Knows Best." (Also a TV series. TV played a major role in forming many of my ideals. Like the good guy wins out, they always find you out if you lie or cheat, parents do not argue or raise their voices, children always mind.)

Another thing I now realize was that in my fantasy the children I reared never got over six or seven years of age. Even when I think of "children" now, I see mostly the positive, and often unrealistic, side of them, and they are always very congenial and under seven.

It is all rather funny. I can laugh about my fantasies now. I can see how unrealistic they were. A baby that would never cry or sass anyone back. All she was going to do was be perfect, sit and smile, and be aggressive only when the occasion called for it, and certainly be well mannered. Not like her brother and sister, who are now twelve and fourteen. And whoever planned to be the parents of adolescents?

I think the oddest thing about being a parent is that you learn as you go and when you get good at it you are all through. Like someone said, "In school you take the lesson and then you take the test; in life you take the test and then you learn the lesson."

This mother, aged forty, with a son aged five, lost two babies in early miscarriage between the birth of her first child and this pregnancy. She underwent amniocentesis in her sixteenth week of pregnancy because of her age and the risk of Down's syndrome in babies produced by older mothers. She received the test results in her twentieth week. When she was informed that her baby did not have any apparent genetic deformities testable before birth, she also requested to know the sex of her unborn baby. It was a boy. This prompted feelings of loss and sadness because she had "expected a girl. I guess I was presumptuous enough to assume you got what you wanted."

Her age and her previous difficulties in carrying babies to term would make this pregnancy her last. She had to work through her feelings of disappointment about not having a daughter. In many ways she was more fortunate than other parents who must wait until the moment of birth to discover the sex of their child and then work out any negative responses. She had a five-month head start on this sometimes painful process.

What were some of the specific fantasies she had about having a daughter?

A boy for you and a girl for me

I had thought for a long time about having a girl—a beautiful baby—dressing her in girl clothes. I have the impression that my feelings about this fantasy baby were different than about a boy baby. I had trouble feeling close to my son the first couple of years. I think this might have something to do with prohibitions of closeness to my male twin, and also to some distinct feelings about fondling and physically loving boy versus girl children. I definitely wanted a boy for my husband and a girl for me, a matched duo. My son's personality is very much like my husband's, and I guess I figured it was my turn now. The thought of three boys and me seemed lopsided somehow. When my son was a little baby I often felt left out. I feel now he is more like me.

My fantasies about having a daughter are very detailed: fantasies about having a daughter who is herself having a baby, being an old woman and having a daughter there for me. I had images of going out with my daughter, buying her dresses and jewelry. When I would see adolescent girls walking down the street, I would wonder what my teenage daughter would look like . . . a lot of my fantasies had to do with what she would look like. I always pictured my daughter as thin, tall, and lithe, with blond hair—all the girls in my family looked like that.

One reaction, after my initial disappointment, was a feeling of relief. Now I can get on with the business of my own life. I think I would have spent all my time with my girl, would have deferred my own life. I would have wanted with a passion to undo all that I had gone through with my own mother. I would blame myself terribly if I didn't meet success, if I had caused my child the same grief. The residual sadness I feel is that loss of the experience of real closeness between a girl and her mother. Not having that with a child makes me most unhappy. But throughout my adult life I have parented many young women—as a teacher, role model, and mother surrogate—and I will have other opportunities to exercise my mothering role.

Creating the perfect child

The myth of the ideal child is one that many parents never give up. We think that if we had the chance to do things differently, our children would have fewer shortcomings. Giving up this myth, at least in part, can help us to feel less overwhelmingly responsible for their lives and to see them as real people. Being aware of our ideal can help furnish us with values, expectations, and an appreciation of our children.

Donna:

One night shortly before the birth of my first child I was disturbed by a thought that happened through my mind. I realized that I had had a negative thought about my baby. I had had negative thoughts before during my pregnancy—about nausea, about my doctor, about what delivery might be like, about going to the bathroom constantly—but this thought brought me up short because the baby was sacred and, I had felt, not a part of any of the realities of pregnancy. The thought which had passed through my mind was that if it weren't for this baby I wouldn't be having to go through enormous pain in a few days. However, it wasn't the content of the thought that bothered me but the feelings. Why should I be shocked at a silly little thought?

I realized that this thought had violated an idea I had about perfection, how I was going to be the perfect mother and, more importantly, make my baby's life as perfect as possible. From conception, and even before, I felt I had loved my baby or the idea of my baby. It felt like he had a beautiful existence in my mind even before he was conceived and this negative thought was a prick on my consciousness like a cactus needle on a smooth finger. I remember Doris Lessing saying in *The Four Gated City* how the mother feels the first time her child falls down and gets a bruise, that something she has created is no longer perfect and never will be again. I had suddenly realized my vulnerability to produce the ideal child.

Such a tremendous ego trip—and yet I realize almost seven years and two children later that this feeling of producing perfection is a stage in becoming a parent. Some people aren't aware of it and never let go of it. But I remember that the awareness of it haunted me from then on and it was a first step in realizing that I was not capable of creating an ideal child, myself as ideal parent, or the world as an ideal experience for him. It was my first real feeling that he would have his own experiences, even of me, and that though I would initially introduce him to many of them it was neither desirable nor possible for me to control them. Not even my thoughts. The world proves this to me every day, but I think back to that first pregnancy as an idyll, a land I will never return to, but necessary somehow, as if the hopes and dreams prepared me in spirit for the day-to-day realities of motherhood.

RENEWAL

Under autumn rain-fed grass
my 6-year-old
found newborn spiders
hundreds of them
swarming their vacant nest
in antic footsteps.

They remind me
of the month-old pony we saw
kicking his rickety legs
at intruders
while his mother ate oats
sedately by his side

Or you my son
driving your bike like a speed racer
down our country road
with my gaze
around you
like a loose lasso
following you from inside
our picture window

and down some hidden pathways
where I run
goalless
jacketless
the sense of cold air on my arms
matched by neighborhood boys
and the headiness
of hard tether ball
and sleds
stretching the day
like a rubber band
to its reluctant end.

SUSAN ISAACS

NOTES

1. Lecture by Ernest Pecci at conference, "Death, Dying, and Beyond," March 1976, John F. Kennedy University, Lafayette, California.
2. Phillip Mitchell, unpublished paper, Education for Living Center, Lafayette, California, 1978.
3. Flora Davis, "Are You Trying to Be Too Good a Parent?" *Redbook*, April 1977, p. 91.
4. Arthur D. and Libby Lee Colman, *Pregnancy: The Psychological Experience* (New York: Seabury Press, 1971), p. 144.
5. Gerald Caplan, *An Approach to Community Mental Health* (New York: Grune and Stratton, 1961), pp. 80–81.
6. John H. Kennell and Marshall H. Klaus, *Maternal-Infant Bonding* (St. Louis: C. V. Mosby, 1976), p. 174.
7. William Kotzwinkle, "Swimmer in the Secret Sea," *Redbook*, July 1974, p. 119.
8. Alice Lake, "Three for the See Saw: How a First Baby Changes a Marriage," *Redbook*, April 1974, p. 150.
9. Angela Barron McBride, *The Growth and Development of Mothers*, pp. 17–18.

3. Giving Birth to the Parent

Mary Bauman's journal entry, August 12, 1974 (two weeks before the birth of her second child):

The complete mystery which requires complete acceptance —a baby—the within-ness. I find that I resent and yet am hypnotized by its control of me and my time and my spirit. These days of waiting until some irrational, primitive machinations bring the secret to a close and the person to a beginning. And for a woman it is hard sometimes not to feel used, and not to feel her self denied—identity shot to hell as though one were a dandelion puff through which a fierce wind blows—a victim, a body, a shell, a shed skin.

I seem to be confronted all around by the Events of life; birth, death, and even that intangible force, love. We know these things happen but are they true? How fully does one have to experience before one really believes/understands? Who is ever ready? I think to understand and to accept death or birth or love are contradictory operations: to understand is to embrace and suffer, to be beyond human limits, while to accept is the livable way—the achievement of reason and "identity" and functioning preservation. I wish that I would know why a baby *is* and what that makes me in the process. Or am I only a process—a summer season?

Birth. At what other time in history has that word stood for a revolution? A revolution in people's awareness, in medical practice, and in the shared experience of husband and wife. A revolution that boasts a new vocabulary as its artillery: Natural Childbirth, Gentle Birth, Prepared Birth, Home Birth, Aware Birth. Some of the terms, only a few years old, are already household words.

Lamaze and Leboyer have become conversational passwords among women of childbearing age. "Are you doing Lamaze?" women ask one another automatically. "Are you having a Leboyer birth?"

It is the knowledge or consciousness that these terms imply which gives them their potency. A great part of the strength women have achieved in the experiences of labor and delivery has come through understanding and having names for each step of that process. It was Marjorie Karmel's knowledge and conviction that birth could be different from the menu of choices the hospitals offered that gave her the courage to let other women hear about the techniques (now considered classic) in the thank you that rocked a generation, *Thank You Dr. Lamaze.* It was the power of her knowledge based on firsthand experience that made women believe her, demand something different in their own experiences, and pass on their stories to other women. Those stories that had always been told in private, about women's events, woman to woman, were suddenly told boldly and with a different theme as a result of that one story about the Lamaze experience that was communicated with such honesty and detail.

There were other revolutionary milestones in this movement, doctors and childbirth educators whose names are also passwords of the new vocabulary, such as Read, Bing, Bradley. Many people have worked to establish new options for women and a new vision of an age-old experience—birth. But Karmel's story, told scarcely twenty years ago, has been a model for the importance of all the individual stories that women since have had the impetus to tell. The new books written on birth in the last few years could fill a bookcase, and perhaps they are so easily marketed because they document a change in consciousness that has even greater significance for men and women than the individual techniques that they describe.

In any case, birth is an issue, and where you stand on it can categorize you in certain circles faster than anything currently political. The issues of hospital versus home birth, of midwives versus doctors, of hospital practices, are endlessly discussed in books, articles, and even TV news programs, not to mention daily conversation. Home birth is even something of a status symbol today, a fact that is ironic when you consider that it was status that originally led women into hospitals. Even women who would never make that choice themselves may look wistfully at their counterparts who give birth in the privacy of their own beds.

The trouble is that as in any revolution, we can get so caught up in its issues and rhetoric that we don't see the real changes occurring in our own perceptions. Perhaps we can get a grasp of our attitudes by looking at the leaders of our revolution and the pictures we have of them. The potency of their effect on us may lie in the very fact that they are ordinary women like ourselves, and so their experience has a definitive relation to our own.

The ordinary woman bearing a child is anything but ordinary. In order to see her clearly now, we have to be able to see how we visualized her in the past—how our pictures of her have changed and what we have invested in seeing her as we do.

Representations of pregnant women abound. She has long been a popular subject for artists and more recently photographers because she evokes such rich imagery. We can tell much about our own visions from these tangible portraits. The book *Family of Man*, based on the historic photo exhibit of the same name in the 1950s, portrays expectant women from many different cultures. One group

of photographs seems especially telling. Three women, all
from the United States, share the same mood, the same
page, the same condition. The largest photo shows a
woman through a foreground of plants, standing in a soft,
flowing nightgown, looking wistfully out a window, the
most Mona Lisa–like of smiles playing on her lips. Under-
neath there is a profile of soft curves—a woman lying on a
bed with a kitten curled under her swollen belly. And the
smallest picture shows a woman with a look that, although
she is surrounded by others, is focused not at the external
world but seemingly on some other vision, perhaps of
future reality.[1]

In Catherine Milinaire's book *Birth,* published in 1974,
the women look directly at us. Their bodies are often un-
clothed, with no soft fabrics to emphasize the roundness
of their maternal conditions. Breasts and swollen bellies
are displayed proudly. These women are not in states of
reverie, though a few communicate that feeling. In many
of the photographs the women's legs are spread and we
see a baby's head emerging from a vagina.[2]

What do these pictures tell us? Have women changed
this radically in a generation, or is it just the boldness of
the photographer seeking new subject matter? Obviously
it would have to be a little of both, but the difference in
the poses, the settings, the attitudes, must finally say something significant about us all.

In the *Family of Man* pictures we see a solitary woman
preoccupied with her condition in a way that seems to exclude in its reverie all others and most especially the everyday world. Her husband and other people in the same
picture are not her focus—we are aware of her dream of
the future. These are pictures to evoke images in us about
what womanhood means, the mysteries, the sisterhood of
all women in their roles as the keepers, the threshold of
life. The pictures do not include any hints for us on individual women and how they have weathered or tran-

scended this transition into motherhood. Pictures of child-birth show women suffering, crying out, their faces in anguish. No women are included for whom birth seemed a peak, something enjoyed or transcended by their own spirits. Our interest in these early pictures of birth and pregnancy seems centered around the beauty and suffering, the poetry, of the human condition.

Today we are shown the individual woman. Her picture tells the story of her triumph. She remains the image of all women in her condition, but she is not just serene, wistful, or anguished. In Milinaire's book we see her as curious, glamorous, sexy, disheveled, sweating, hardworking, excited, ecstatic, solitary, and involved with others. We see the man as an integral part of the whole process. We don't see her labor as just a painful event best hidden and forgotten. We see it, rather, in all its stages and in many different settings. We see it in great detail and photographed from a multitude of angles—the effects of labor on her body, the baby's head first "crowning" in the vagina, then head emerging, shoulders emerging, the baby being caught, held, having its cord cut, being nursed, massaged, and held in warm water, the finishing touch.

We see the human condition through the lens of individual achievement and experience. This experience is captured not so much to provoke our imagery as to instruct. Woman giving woman the steps, the "how to" of every detail of breath, the options of bodily position, the techniques, the sensations, the attitudes, the importance of help provided by husband and/or others supporting her in her work.

The How-To:
· of feeling ecstasy rather than fear
· of giving birth in your own individual way
· of flowing with and participating in the intensity of the experience

- of using discipline and control
- of using education to understand your own physical process
- of using mates and others for support and help
- of wielding your choice to get what you want out of the experience
- of continuing throughout birth the togetherness out of which the child was conceived

This comprehensive portrayal is a symbol of woman measuring herself and her own abilities to shape her experience, rather than being defined by it. The very displaying of her birth is somehow part of the process which says that her life doesn't have to be hidden or clandestine. It has become integral to her self-esteem.

If we want to know our own future, how we will photograph woman a generation from now, we should take a look at these pictures and see what they say about us. Perhaps all we can do here is to raise some questions that will help us to observe the changes we are participating in more closely. Of course, the real trick in observing, as we mentioned earlier, is not our ability to see the details, but to be aware of the developing pattern.

Looking at this modern woman, we might ask ourselves who she is. Is her story a romantic one? The romance has changed its emphasis over the years—lost its sensitiveness —but in the triumph, the joy, the love, and the radiance, the romance is most definitely there.

Maybe we need to ask ourselves if all birth is romantic. For women who do not want the child they are carrying, who give birth to a child of the "wrong" sex, a baby that they are not equipped to handle, a handicapped or stillborn baby, the pictures are not as appealing. Dr. Henry Kempe, a pioneer in the treatment of child abuse, has filmed the reactions of mothers to their babies right after birth and has documented a variety of reactions ranging from joy to disgust, depending on the woman's feelings toward herself and the event.[3] Is there a danger of seeing birth itself as infinitely romantic in its possibilities by ignoring the life backgrounds, feelings, and expectations that women bring to it? Or of thinking the event is a peak experience for everyone, when for some it may have a wholly different significance?

For the woman who wants her baby, who prepares, and who involves her mate in the whole process of pregnancy, labor, and delivery, is the triumphant birth a test by which she measures her womanhood? If the testee and the tester are one, the woman herself, what happens if she finds herself wanting? How is her self-esteem affected? Her relations with her spouse or baby?

It would be very difficult to estimate the number of mothers who have attempted natural childbirth through one method or another. Many have picked up one of the dozen books on the subject which detail the glowing experience of other women having painless, fearless, joyful births. Many women have attended at least a few natural childbirth classes, and some have gone all the way into the hospital on their husband's arm, proudly announcing to all the staff that they have attended a natural birth course. But while a few women in America may have experienced an un-drugged birth, practically no one has experienced a truly natural birth.[4]

If this assessment is accurate, there are two questions we might pose. First, how do these women who go in with such high expectations feel about themselves if they don't compare with those "glowing women"? Second, who has defined the standards for "natural birth"?

In her book *Immaculate Deception,* Suzanne Arms points out that obstetricians have a wide variety of definitions of what natural childbirth is. She herself defines it in a different way. It becomes clear that the vocabulary of the childbirth movement which has achieved such popularity and power does not necessarily have clear definitions yet, and the pictures they conjure up in us can, if unfulfilled, have negative consequences. "What has led to a 'hope' that fully expects failure is the high number of disappointed women who have attempted natural birth in hospitals and found that having a baby hurt like hell, that medication helped, and that the 'joy' of natural childbirth was either a lie or an impossible dream."[5]

Arms blames this failure on the negative attitudes and parentalism of the medical profession. Maybe that answer is too simple. As women, we have contributed to disappointment by predicting too glowing a picture of childbirth. Maybe we have cast too much blame on the medical profession and have not taken a look at the variety of motivations, feelings, and backgrounds that women bring to the experience.

Catherine Milinaire has said that the answer to our fears about birth is facing them and talking about them. However, the women we see giving birth in her book do not look fearful. We are told that childbirth isn't painful, that there is nothing to be afraid of. What happens if afterward a woman feels duped? If she is not able to exercise control? What if something goes wrong and nature proves her vulnerable rather than in charge and triumphant? Does it matter whom we cast blame on then? What responsibilities do women need to take to approach our experiences, so that birth does not result in an identity crisis?

The implications are greater than we might think. Studies have shown that the way a woman perceives her labor and delivery affects her feelings toward mothering. Mothers who feel birth was hard are more likely to want their babies fed by bottle and cared for in the nursery. Women who have positive feelings about birth are more apt to want to breast-feed and to look after their babies themselves. "Women who had uterine inertia often refused to have another child. The fact that psychoses are precipitated by childbirth gives further indication that childbirth is a very potent experience."[6]

It might help if we individualized our education to include counseling that would help women to deal with their feelings about the birth experience and about parenting. If our feelings about birth can be influenced by what we have been educated to believe, we have to be careful that our educational techniques include broad definitions of the experience. We must allow women to talk about their fantasies and fears. Many childbirth educators feel it is important for women to hear stories that reveal the diversity of individual experience.

Two contrasting observations on childbirth:

"I was taking a Lamaze class. It wasn't going to hurt to have the baby. My mother kept telling me not to believe them. It would hurt—and it did. Even though it did, it was still the finest experience of my life, to give birth to a healthy child."

"It is now well established that if you prepare carefully and are in good health, there is rarely any suffering involved in pregnancy and childbirth."[7]

How are we to reconcile these two radically different points of view? It is true that radiant childbirth cannot be achieved with fear of pain and that fear can make childbirth more painful. So we try not to elicit fear. Childbirth educators have learned, however, that to tell women there is no pain can result in anger in women after birth, toward people who perpetrated what they feel is a lie, or toward their husband, or toward themselves.

Women experience a wide spectrum of pain in childbirth, from almost no sensation to suffering that some find hard to endure. The challenge is finding ways to make every woman confident to meet her child, no matter how easy or stressful, fearful or radiant her birth.

The pivotal question is whether we want to place a heavy, long-term emphasis on the birth process itself. Historically, bringing to awareness the choices available to women and working to change attitudes in society—

specifically in the medical profession—have been important stages in the development of parental consciousness—a transition, we might ask, delivering us to what? "From the standpoint of investment of time and thought, it seems unbalanced to spend the days of pregnancy preparing for childbirth when it is parenthood with which we will be largely concerned from the moment of delivery on."[8]

Parents who experience natural and even radiant births report, generally, the same problems and confusions with their children as other parents do. They may call them by different names, or ascribe different meanings to them, but the crises people experience during parenting are remarkably similar, no matter how unique they seem to us. On the other hand, some of the people who report the most joy out of parenting have given birth under the most trying conditions. It is dangerous to see our effectiveness as parents linked to one experience. It may be that a radiant birth propels us into parenthood with more exuberance and self-esteem. Certainly the period of pregnancy and birth is a time of growth, but that does not mean we do not grow when things turn out differently than we expected, when our plans for birth are turned upside down. Who is to say which experience is the better teacher? The question is how every parent can, regardless of background, expectations, and experiences enter parenthood feeling happy and confident.

Pregnancy itself is a time of new definitions. Our changing bodies force us to reevaluate who we are, as does the life we feel growing within us. It is a time of more fluid consciousness, when unconscious images and archaic and unfamiliar feelings can flood our rational perceptions of ourselves. To approach pregnancy in a rigidly defined way is to deny the message that our unconscious minds are giving us. Explore. Redefine. Regress. Build. This is a time for developing new patterns of thinking in women and men and for recognizing feelings that will be both highly individual and universal. Can we allow ourselves to be as aware of our own inner changes as we have become of the stages and vocabulary of labor and delivery?

Is the reason we have focused on the nine months of pregnancy as a preparation for conscious birth rather than conscious parenthood because it makes parenthood somehow more definable and less overwhelming? If we do this, then we want to be assured that such and such will follow. In fact, there are just such ideas of cause and effect attached to the mystique of birth and its effects on our abilities as parents. It is such assumptions about prepared birth, natural birth, home birth, and even nursing that can distort our view of parenting as a process.

There is an implicit assumption that people who take part in natural childbirth make better parents and even produce better babies. Correlated with this belief is the myth of the superbaby who will come out of the new birth experiences. The danger of these assumptions becomes more obvious when we turn them around. Parents who fall short of natural childbirth won't be as good at parenting. Babies who are the victims of a less than completely natural birth or who aren't nursed or are not allowed to stay with their mothers afterward are likely to be less alert and less psychologically well adjusted. The frightening implications of these assumptions come from the mouths of parents themselves more and more frequently, it seems. "I'm not as close to that child," they quite often say. "I'm sure it's because he was born in the hospital," "because I didn't nurse him," "because he was taken away right after birth." Who can blame parents for wanting to make their experiences more simple and understandable when life presents us with such complexity? Parents want to feel that their very positive experiences of natural birth, of nursing, of closeness afterward, have deep meaning (which they do). They want the things they do to have some kind of magic that will insure them against the suffering and self-doubt they see in parents so often in the world around them. However, these simplistic assumptions can be convenient formulas for trying to fit the complex relationships and feelings that go into parenting into an equation we can handle.

This kind of thinking can result in a psychological inertia which allows the parent to rationalize rather than to work at the difficulties of the relationship. For example, many women are slow to warm up to their babies. It is not uncommon for real attachment to begin with these women as late as six months, a year, or later. One woman told us, "I feel I had difficulty in establishing a bond with my second daughter. It took sixteen months to feel close to her—she and Johnny were much closer. She would call John Mommy—she wouldn't be comforted by me. By sixteen months we were finally ready to relate. We held each other one day for seven hours. We were OK."

If we are given the convenient option that it is the kind of birth that determines our feelings rather than the natural confusion of entering a new role, then that natural awakening may never occur. Many women need to work at a relationship with a child to feel a real bond, and the easy answer that our style of birth rather than our individual makeup determines how we feel may be a deterrent to the growth of positive feelings. If all of us start to accept the fact that our desire for easy answers is a deterrent to our growth, and if we see that all relationships, even with a child, take hard work, then we will have the foundation for being better parents.

We should remember to include our old pictures in the ever changing album that portrays our visions of pregnancy, birth, and parenthood. In the wonderfully detailed book *Pregnancy: The Psychological Experience*, the Colmans make allusions to old pictures: "Photographers and painters have captured this state best when they show the pregnant woman standing serenely at a window, emphasizing the extent to which her experiential world is taking place on the inside, but with a reminder that it is on the brink of making the transition, of passing through the window into the world beyond."[9]

We need that awareness of the transition, the ways that we relate to pregnancy and what we are looking toward, perhaps as much as we need the "how to"—the pictures that educate us about the physical and feeling process.

The natural childbirth movement is a powerful model and tool for ways in which we can help each other as well as ourselves. Let us incorporate those huge strides we have made into the broader picture of what it means to be a parent.

Interviews

The role of preparation

Where can we go to get support and guidance for more than childbirth? Who can help us to prepare to become the parents we want to be?

Q.: Did you have any picture before the birth of what your child would be like?

Gail, age 34; three children, ages 8, 2½, newborn:

I was probably as much a believer in the myth of, you know, the nice little six-month-old you get to see in all the commercials, the myth that it would be all wonderful, not in terms of, oh, this would bring this relationship together, but it would be really enriching. I think we were very caught up in this myth. But I don't think this society prepares anyone for parenthood. I went to the La Leche League before she was born, from the fifth month on, so I was at least prepared for what that was all about, and we went to Lamaze classes. For us it was the challenge of Lamaze rather than the baby. We were into making it with no help, and having the baby was anti-climactic. Oh, well, there's the baby! We were so up when it happened, we were at the pinnacle of highs. Everything after that was downhill. We were so wound up all those months before.

Home birth as self-expression

Our values and personal myths influence our experience of childbirth when we have the power to exercise some important options.

> **Brigid, mother of three children, two born at home and one in the hospital, ages 8, 3, 7 months:**
>
> I really liked Bradley [a technique for birth]. It fit more the way I felt about childbirth. It wasn't contrived. It sort of seemed like what people would just do naturally without any training if they were relaxed. I didn't feel like I needed to do anything else in childbirth than what came naturally. That's why I liked home birth, because I didn't feel I needed to go anywhere or do anything to have my baby. I think the main reason I wanted to have her at home was that I didn't want anyone else to handle her or be near her. It was my business to take care of her. She grew inside me and I knew how to take care of her. They took Mani away for eight hours after she was born and that was a crime. The bonding studies have proved that. My mother had my brother at home in Austria. She had me in a hospital but with a midwife. But the atmosphere in the hospitals is much more loving there.

The crucial role of support

How can we use our experiences to benefit other parents and to help professionals to understand our needs?

> **Frances; two children, ages 6, 4:**
>
> I am convinced from the births of my first and second children that the length of labor, the supportiveness of individuals around you, and your own reaction to

labor affects your feelings of competence as a mother.

My first labor was very long. I was in false labor for one day before real labor began. I didn't eat because it felt real to me so I was already weak when it got heavier. I had taken Lamaze and I felt it was invaluable to me. I never missed a breath during my whole labor. I had practiced regularly but I was absolutely amazed at my capacity to keep up the breathing. The nurses kept saying I would hyperventilate but I never did. When the pain felt too much I took medication. The attitude of the nurses or my own reaction was that the pain and duration of labor was my fault. When it came to pushing I pushed for two hours and had a black eye afterward.

The next day I was exhausted. I wanted my baby but after twenty-two hours of labor all I could do was sleep. When I brought him home from the hospital I found nursing painful and didn't know who to ask for help. I called La Leche League and they gave me much advice which I followed religiously. My baby still cried with hunger all the time. I was away from family. At a month the doctor said he hadn't gained enough. I decided to quit nursing. I had never failed at anything so important to me. It took months for me to get over it.

With my second baby, her labor was six hours. My husband didn't believe I was in labor. It was all so easy. After she was born I had so much energy. I could walk around, take a shower, talk on the phone. My roommate in the hospital was a first mother and was too tired to even hold her baby even though she had rooming-in. It seemed the nurses were rather abrupt with her. Her husband had wanted a boy and she felt bad that it was a girl. I was amazed at the difference in our energy, having felt just as exhausted as she did the first time.

I was in a special hospital program where we went

home from the hospital early and the nurse visited us at home. I had some of the same sensations in nursing but, lo and behold, when the nurse would come to my house she showed me how to nurse, told me nothing was wrong, and her encouragement and knowledge made me successful. In fact I nursed for fifteen months.

Common misconceptions

Our stories of birth don't have to be radiant ones in order for us to communicate something important to one another. Talking about changes in our expectations and attitudes can help others to benefit from the same process.

Mary Beth, age 20:

I took Lamaze classes and I really went in with the attitude that there would be no pain. I thought, I know what to do. We didn't practice enough. We enjoyed the classes—being with a bunch of other pregos. I had no fear. The last class we saw a movie on natural childbirth and I thought, That's the way it will be. She was doing great.

I had a rude awakening. He was ten days early. I wasn't prepared. I woke up at five A.M. and thought I was wetting the bed. I finally realized what was happening and called my doctor. He had left for Mexico for the weekend. The answering service gave me another doctor, an older doctor. He said to come in to the emergency room. I still had no contractions.

He checked me. The water had broken and there was three centimeters dilation. At noon I still had no contractions. The doctor finally came in. I kept listening to the deliveries; it was really neat, there was no fussing. I thought, This is going to be neat. He examined me and said he would break the membranes. I still thought there would be no pain. I had one hard, heavy contraction. I wasn't prepared. I told the nurse to call my husband who had gone home to sleep as I thought he should rest since I didn't need him. When he came I was doing the breathing. The contractions were irregular. They kept getting worse. The breathing wasn't doing anything but it gave me something to think about.

It got to a point. They had advised us to do all these things, eat ice chips, et cetera. He would try to help me and I would smack his hands and say don't touch me. I went into transition. I was flipping around from side to side; he had to run from one side of the bed to the other. I would slap his hands and yell at him and sometimes he would look at me like I was the devil incarnate.

Finally it was time to push. The doctor said to push with each contraction. Three girls came in and left for the delivery. At times it seemed like a torture chamber. I wish I could have screamed but I didn't have the strength. I pushed for two or three hours. I was delirious. There was a girl next to me who wouldn't push. The doctor kept yelling at her that she had to push or the baby wouldn't come out. I was pushing my guts out. During transition I had to have a shot. I would panic and Tony would say breathe, breathe. It was like one big, long transition. At six the doctor came in. I said, "I can't push anymore." He took me in and gave me a saddleblock.

If I had to give any advice I would say to practice the Lamaze more. I wouldn't have panicked if I had practiced more. I really went in thinking no pain. I felt disillusioned with the teacher who said, "We don't call it pain—just contractions." I was kind of shocked. It was harder on me to be slapped with reality. I

wouldn't want to scare people *but I would want them
to face reality.*

Shared beginnings

We have to start to look at the hours after birth as the
beginning of a relationship, not just the end of pregnancy
or labor. Sometimes when our babies are kept away from
us we can feel as if we don't know them after going home.
We can have the vague sense for a while that they belong
to the hospital staff and are only with us on loan.

Gretchen:

I felt secure real fast. The first night at home he cried.
It was the first time I had ever heard him cry. In the
hospital he had always been behind glass. *I had never
seen him cry.* I think it was all the people who had
come over to see him. My mom. I really wanted to be
alone with him. I sat with him in my room alone. He
calmed right down.

Catherine, mother of three children:

We got to keep our baby with us this time after her
birth. It was so wonderful. She never left us. We re-
covered together. The nurse stayed with us in the
recovery room and did all the tests. I was amazed at
how alert she was, and calm. How she looked right in
my eyes. And the nurse said well, the other ones were
that way too but you just didn't see them because
they were in the nursery. I sure have noticed a difference with her. She is so calm, strong, active. I think
maybe because she wasn't passed between a lot of
people. Her beginnings were just what I would
ideally want them to be, which gives me such a sense
of well-being.

Growth and development of fathers

What does a man gain from watching and aiding in the birth process? We can be changed by the qualities of empathy and nurturance that emerge from such an experience.

> **Gordon, age 35; child, age 8:**
>
> That's why I have empathy for a woman. I think it gave more closeness to me and to Marti, my daughter. I couldn't participate or carry Marti within my own body; the next best thing I could do was be close to the action and be there. And being as calm as I could be. Even then I felt it was my child. I wanted to reach out and hold her, even covered with afterbirth. When I saw her head come out I wanted to hold her. Afterward I was as close as I could be to my baby. I spent a good deal of time with her. Sometimes when my wife wanted to get away I would keep her even for the whole weekend.

Perhaps the new role of father in our society begins in the delivery room. The experience of being needed and involved in such a vital way sets a model for the rest of parenthood.

> **Pat, father of two children:**
>
> When Joan was pregnant, I sometimes wished I were the pregnant one so I could feel all she was feeling; other times I felt cut off from her in this experience. I didn't feel the pains and frustrations as keenly.
>
> Being in the delivery room was a real thrilling experience—an all-time great. I saw the baby crown before she did. She couldn't see it and that was hysterical, getting her to see what I already could. I felt very useful there, since she had back labor and

was already too numb to feel the final contractions. I could feel her and tell when to push.

Being your own midwife

Hearing about a parent's experience in another culture can give us better insights into our own.

Maria, aged fifty-four, has nine children, seven grand-children. A Mexican-American born in Texas and raised in Minnesota, she met her husband in Guadalajara at seventeen and got married. She had her first baby at eighteen. She delivered her own children and worked as a midwife in Mexico for hundreds of families. She stayed twenty-three years in Mexico and then came to the United States.

Maria:

We moved to Michuacan when we got married. There were about five hundred people in 1939. The beds were covered with straw. They had to carry water in pots. They would kill a cow once a week. After raising us in Minnesota my mom had moved back there as my aunts were there and we moved there to be near them. I didn't speak Spanish and my husband didn't speak English. When I was eighteen I was going to have a baby and my aunt who was ninety came to stay with us for a few days. Finally she got tired and left for home. My mother was with me when I had the child. Afterward I got fever and was in bed for fifty-five days. They even made a coffin for me and dug the hole. My mother took care of my baby while I was sick. That baby died after two months of whooping cough. I cried for over two years until I had the second one.

My second baby was born in the hospital but I

delivered him. The nurse wouldn't believe me. She was washing some things and by the time she came back with the doctor I was holding him and the cord was broken. My other babies, except for the last, were born at home. With my seventh one the doctor had said that there was something wrong so I had to have it in the hospital. I started contractions at seven in the morning. I got up and sent my fifteen-year-old off to work. I was nervous because I was embarrassed. We never told them we were pregnant. He said, "Are you sick? I'm going to get Dad." My husband came and the contractions were five minutes apart. He went to get a cab. Taxis were slow. I went into the shower then drank some manzanita tea. The contractions came faster! I went downstairs and got my things that I used as a midwife out of the trunk. I had the baby before they got back. Now she's seventeen and the mother of our household.

The last one was born in the hospital but he came out while I was just sitting up.

One time my four-year-old came in when one of my babies was being born. That was the fastest baby. I was so embarrassed. I told him to go in the other room. He told everyone later that I had gone potty in the bed.

Nowadays my daughter has diapers. I had to make my diapers and all their clothes. I was also a wet nurse for three or four children. The families were rich and didn't want the mother to nurse.

With my last baby I lost my milk. There is a belief that if you take a bath right away and your back gets cold the milk dries. A neighbor said I didn't have enough milk. She mixed chocolate with olive oil and cumin seeds. She ground them and put them on my back warm with an old sheet until the next day. It was so dry and sticky. I had to stay in bed for three days. Afterward I had so much milk I nursed her and one other baby.

I used to cook apples and carrots and grind them. I used to put liver in drinking alcohol and leave it a day and grind it. I started to give them tastes of everything I was eating at a month. I nursed for about a year. I would lie down and take turns nursing them. Being a midwife, I was always busy. If I had to go out I would leave them in the playpen with toys; the older ones took care of the younger ones.

I never got up with my babies at night. They never cried at night from the time they were born. One did once when my mother had a stroke. I gave him whiskey with water and sugar. I would swaddle them and tie them around. My mother taught me as a girl. I was the oldest of twelve. I would help her with the babies. I never knew when my mother was going to have a baby even when I was seventeen. I believe the more children you have, the healthier you are. I go to dances, I jump around now.

Margo, age 39; two children, ages 16, 8:

I wasn't really excited about having kids but when I had the most beautiful babies in the whole world it came as quite a surprise. A baby is a real joy. I think childbirth is great. It was one of the most wonderful experiences of my life. I wasn't looking forward to a baby and then it was like I was suddenly overwhelmed. There's all the mother love that God sends you. I wasn't prepared for those feelings.

THE FIRST HOURS WITH EMILY
(*The First Loss*)

We had a special thing,
A mystical bond,
In the beginning.

She knew all
and I knew what every cry meant.

She looked into my eyes,
Her stare penetrated deep inside.
I saw my grandmother
And she stared back at me.

And then it was broken.
A lot of pushing and sticking,
Formulas, mucus tubes, bottles, nipples . . .
Maybe it was inevitable,
After all, the real world is harsh,
Unlike the womb.

I cried
I couldn't protect her.
Would she ever trust me again,
So perfectly,
So naturally—
I think not.

JOAN ALEXANDER WEINSTEIN

Are we simply bulging sacks warming the unborn
who grow in our cocoons like weighty butterflies
kicking and knocking to come out,
dragging us to the threshold of pain?

Are we slaves thinking every meal a sacrifice,
every dirty scattered sock an affront
to our queenly pride, our breaking backs?
This I would say is our delusion.

Did not God make us thus?
Did we not choose this life,
this mastery in servitude?

When we but remember to forget ourselves
we are the nameless ones,
his belly and his hands raising
pruned trees for the garden.

And mothers are blessed
with a hint from the divine.
Ask yourself—who is this really
who has come from inside your very womb

to cry out in the night,
to sigh at your breast.
Who is this helpless form,
this breath of light

who lies in his cradle
and trusts you will awaken
in him his very self:
an open shimmering heart.

JAN KAPLAN
April 2, 1978

NOTES

1. *Family of Man,* Museum of Modern Art by MACO Magazine Co., 1955, pp. 18–19.
2. Catherine Milinaire, *Birth* (New York: Harmony Books, Crown Publishers, 1974).
3. Henry Kempe, kinescope, "Mothers, Newborn Interaction Film," 1974, University of Colorado Medical Center, Denver, Colorado.
4. Suzanne Arms, *Immaculate Deception* (Boston: Houghton Mifflin, 1975), p. 139.
5. *Ibid.,* p. 140.
6. Niles Newton, *Maternal Emotions* (New York: Harper & Row, 1971), p. 36.
7. Milinaire, *Birth,* p. 72.
8. Polly Berrien Berends, *Whole Child, Whole Parent,* p. 29.
9. Arthur D. and Libby Lee Colman, *Pregnancy,* p. 59.

4. Making Room for the Parent Within Us

The bags I packed eleven years ago were filled with all the wrong things. I was so busy packing, I didn't notice the rules of the game, and even the destination. I put my two feet down and spread my arms in space. I still feel frightened by this emerging freedom of choice. I'm still groping for those role models that were set before me like coloring books where I could stay within the lines.[1]

These words were written by a woman who is piecing together her identity within the role of wife and mother at a time when she finds "the old navigational charts have been tossed," when the coloring-book-sharp definition of a mother's role and a woman's identity has been replaced by a blank page with the potential for an ever changing and individualized design.

The bags she packed when she embarked on her journey into marriage and motherhood probably contained several often contradictory pictures of what lay ahead. As discussed in the chapter on personal myths, she carried one picture of her ideal parent formed by observations of her own parents and popular media figures, and another of the changes she would bring to her role. She also took along a self-portrait of how she saw herself as a whole person apart from any one role in her life—her identity.

Once she became a mate and then a parent, she realized how jumbled her baggage was, how unusable some of its contents. She was faced with the task of sorting out who she really was. She had to develop a realistic picture of her own style of mothering and of her own children, and also had to continue to be aware of and to nurture her identity as part of and something apart from her changing role as a mother.

Just as defining our "dependent role," that role directly tied to our occupation as a parent, is an ongoing process spanning our child-raising years, so is the discovery and maintenance of our *independent role,* which William Glasser, in his book *The Identity Society* defines as that role—not necessarily a career role—which leads us to a "happy, successful, pleasurable belief in ourselves and our own humanity."[2]

Glasser observes that since we no longer have to bear and raise children in order to survive (in few instances do we depend upon our offspring to work our farms or man our businesses), and since the various and widely available birth control methods give us a real choice about starting and continuing pregnancies, people *elect* to raise families. One of the most compelling reasons for raising a family is to help maintain and extend our identities by taking on the new roles as mother and father.

In our search for a tangible and involved personal role, many of us hit upon parenthood as one answer to the question, "Who am I?" Glasser isolates involvement as a necessary prerequisite for a successful independent role or identity. As Glasser writes, child raising offers us a means of direct involvement with others in our interdependence with our children and our mates. It offers us the opportunity to validate our belief in our own human worth by the effect we can have on our children's total physical and emotional growth. We enter into parenthood with hopes of experiencing success in this new role—raising healthy and well-adjusted children—which in turn allow us to feel competent, another vital element in building an identity. And we anticipate situations of shared pleasure and delight introducing our children to the world.

GENERATIVITY: Concern for establishing and guiding the next generation. When this concern is not directed into parental drive or altruistic concerns, or creativity . . . [we see] regression to an obsessive need for pseudo-intimacy, stagnation, boredom, and inter-personal impoverishment.[3]

Erikson specifies no age for the onset of this stage of adult development. What he does make clear is that the formation of identity *precedes* our capacity to be truly intimate with others or to play a parenting role. Becoming a mother or a father provides us with the opportunity to strengthen that identity and to give maximum expression to those parts of ourselves that are concerned with nurturing, guiding, and being intimate with others. We should not, however, mistake it for the only role that can provide us with this opportunity. Nor should we blame parenthood for not providing us with a clear picture of who we are.

What parenthood will offer us is a sense of perspective. Some people, of course, do not experience identity confusion, either in or out of their parenting role. The very real growing pains described in this chapter, however, are not signs that for those of us who do find occasional discomfort it is parenthood itself or our performance as mothers or fathers that is lacking. These are only signals that we are in fact growing and that our definitions of ourselves and of our roles are calling out for renewal or expansion.

Anxiety about maintaining a sense of our nonparent self is felt at differing times in our parenting years. For some, this process occurs even before they have children. One pregnant woman worried:

I'll have a five-month maternity leave from the library after the baby is born, but I'm not sure I should, or really want to, go back to work. I've really gotten all the satisfaction I want out of doing this job, but I remember one year when my husband was working all day and I had no job. I found myself sleeping all the time. I know I'll be busier than I was then with a new baby, but will I also be crazy? Will I lose my direction?

This woman became a parent in her late twenties at a time when she was clearly dissatisfied with the limitations of her career and the boundaries of her personal involvements. Having a baby gave her the opportunity to take on a new occupation and a change in life-style. She could stay home for the first time in five years. But she was also realistically anticipating some discontinuity and sense of loss.

We may undergo this particular adult crisis of identity—that sense of submersion in a single role, of incompleteness—when integral aspects of our personality lie dormant. While one mother experiences this prenatally, another may coast along for years with a genuine feeling of well-being and integration and then suddenly plunge. One mother who had not previously felt any loss of self or confusion about her identity found herself desolate when her daughter started public school:

I always knew who I was—I thought—and where I was going, in terms of my child. I stayed in my home and cared for her, and did day care for other people's children so I could be there for Emily instead of outside working for somebody else. . . . I knew I was good with babies. Everyone told me I was. I felt real good about that part of my life. And then lately, sometimes I feel that all I get strokes for is the nurturing side of me. I know there's more to me than that but it's hard to find when I'm always in a mothering kind of role. Now my daughter is going out of the home into a wider world. What about me? Where am I going?

In this instance we find a parent who proceeded straight from a liberal arts college education and a couple of unsatisfying secretarial jobs into motherhood, with little or no time for discovering or exercising some of her nonnurturing skills. Nonetheless, for a considerable length of time this role involved an important aspect of her identity. As her daughter began to participate in a wider world than her mother had created for her, this mother began to experience a sense of inner claustrophobia similar to that, as she put it, "of a child who must stay inside during a snowstorm. The child can create a little world for herself for a period of time, begin to feel almost comfortable not ever going outside, and then begin to miss—and then absolutely need—to do some of those things you can only do outside."

A gateway to identity

We might assume that the longer we wait before becoming a parent, and the more opportunities for exploring ourselves in a variety of contexts, the more solid our sense of identity and the less possibility for crisis. It is true, conversely, that for teenage parents or very young adults certainly, the task of establishing their identity separate from their children is especially difficult. For young people who are trying on and discarding various new roles, testing out who they are independent of their family and childhood roles, parenthood often appeals as a way of breaking away from old patterns and of finding an instant occupational role. According to Erikson, "Occupational experiences which confirm a person's competence are the most important, even more important than finding a group role, sex role, or world view."[4] "In general," says Edward Pohlman, "it is the inability to settle on an occupational identity which most disturbs young people."[5]

The real fear of not being ready to handle the world of adults yet a desperate need to break out of childhood can make pregnancy especially appealing to a teenager with unhappy family relationships or trouble with peers.

One of the reasons that young women in their teens undertake pregnancies is to prove *they can do something,* and having babies is an option available to them, regardless of education or career preparation. It gives her a clear identity. Motherhood may be a very satisfying occupation, but it is also one behind which all those fears of not measuring up in the outside world can be hidden.[6]

From the outside, becoming pregnant can seem like an instant ticket to adulthood with all its freedoms and privileges. Having a baby to care for can literally, through financial assistance programs to low-income women with dependent children, pay a young woman's way out of her parents' house into her own apartment, with all the initial excitement and challenge of housekeeping and nest building.

However, as the adolescent parent soon discovers, being a parent utilizes and fulfills only a part of our human potential and is a hazardous and unpredictable occupation, filled with detours, roadblocks, and few instant rewards. At a time in their lives when teenagers use loved ones and peers as mirrors of what they are and want to be, a small child can throw back a frustrating and unsatisfactory reflection. If they don't like what they see, if they become bored with or depressed by parenthood, young parents are faced with the fact that a baby is a permanent addition to their lives, unlike a job, best friend, or mentor they can outgrow.

Having a baby can seem like a dramatic way for an adolescent to demonstrate to her parents that she has an approach to parenting that will spare her child the pains of growing up. What very young parents are often really seeking is a tangible affirmation of their own growth and the insights they are gaining as they develop into adults.

Young parents especially need wise and supportive counsel in their efforts to separate clearly their very fluid identities from those of their children. A real potential for crisis exists when the parent sees her child as a mirror image, and when, unhappy with what she sees reflected, she lashes out at her baby or punishes herself.

The search for the ideal age

We brought up the assumption earlier that the longer we wait before becoming parents, the easier our period of adjustment will be. We will have taken the time to develop our careers and other interests. We will have come into parenthood with all the knowledge we've gained from our life experiences. Nonetheless, seasoned adults who decide to have children only after careful, even belabored, consideration of their needs and role definitions may find themselves ill-prepared for the transition and struggling for air.

The very fact that the more mature parent has waited before undertaking this role, making a judicious decision as to the best time, points to one of the flaws in this particular strategy. Parenthood, by this time, may have taken on gigantic proportions in terms of filling holes in or changing the course of an elaborately contrived life master plan.

For the parent who has planned so carefully and who has seen having children as a crucial step in cementing her identity, the always less than perfect reality of parenthood may be devastating. If parenthood is not the answer to her feeling of incompleteness, then where will she find it? Now that she has a child—and she wants to be a conscientious parent—will she have the time left to explore other possibilities? She may discover she has more elaborate dreams to give up and less time to put off unmet needs than a younger parent.

In contrast, the younger mother may have fewer expectations for herself or the role of parent, but also less experience to draw upon and sustain her. She may sometimes feel that she has missed her opportunity to explore other careers and roles. In a supportive framework she can find the saving patience to pace herself in her role testing. If she can develop a perspective on time and realize that the parenting role does indeed eventually end, she can be more relaxed about deferring plans and dreams. She will be less anxious about the roles she might be exploring if she weren't a mother and about the limitations that parenthood might place on her freedom and independence.

"Parenthood, as well as marriage, may need everyone to be at least willing to try on traditional roles for size from time to time."[7] If there are times when parenthood fits too tightly, it also features the comfort of satisfying relationships.

Of course, there is no perfect age for becoming a parent. There are advantages and disadvantages at all our ages and stages, and we follow our own developmental course. Whether a parent is younger or older, her expectations of how parenthood would enhance her identity play a crucial role in her disappointment or contentment with her life. Looking at our pictures again can refresh our awareness of where we came from and where we had hoped to go.

House father: changes without a shake-up

No matter how centered we think we are, parenthood requires a marked time/space adjustment. We might liken entering parenthood to the story of Alice falling into Wonderland. It is a little like going through a door that looks very familiar on the outside into an environment that is so all-absorbing that we can forget very quickly who we were on the other side. Everything, including the people around, takes on a new perspective.

This is especially true for the parent who has the major responsibility for the care of the new child. The amazing

thing is that to the childless around us, the tasks of parenthood still appear very ordinary. The cynical comment
often made by parents in reference to the uninitiated's
romanticized view of parenthood and children is, "If they
only knew." It isn't that what they don't know is something entirely negative. It's just that it looks and feels so
different, and it's so hard to communicate it to them from
a parent's changed perspective.

Jerome Brumbaugh postponed fatherhood until his mid-
forties, following years of strenuous psychotherapy and a
rich professional career. A short time into this new experience, he found himself in the role of daytime caretaker
when he lost his job and his wife found a higher-paying
position.

I never realized what hard, exhausting, energy-depleting
work taking care of children is. It isn't like an avocation, something you can do at the same time as what you were trained
to do, like any kind of intellectual work. It isn't like a regular
nine-to-five job where you can come home and still go downstairs and do woodworking or whatever. It was for me,
especially at first, a complete daily drain. I did not expect that.

Gradually he found ways and time for a continuation of
a professional life in addition to full-time parenting. He
placed his children in a nursery for a period each day while
he pursued other, academic interests. He found time in the
evening and on the weekends, while his wife took the boys
on outings, to exercise other parts of himself that were
critical to his feeling of self-worth. His shock came primarily from anticipating a certain amount of time and energy
expenditure and finding far more required than in any
of his previous occupational roles. His basic sense of himself, his appraisal of his intellectual competence, patience,
and fairness, remained unshaken.

With all of my kids, I have felt distanced from my wife—
other than that I have sensed no inward changes in terms of my
own sense of identity. I felt prepared emotionally for my new

role. I don't change my basic speed in any of my roles; I use the same skills in setting limits for myself and my children and for the people I work with—and also in recognizing my needs.

I feel that fathers and mothers do fill different roles in a family. I have always been around for a large part of the day with all my children—and currently I am actually the main caretaker for my boys while I am unemployed and my wife works full-time. So it is not the physical tasks that I think are different . . . mothers are something special, especially to their sons. And it's not just things like breast-feeding . . . a mother has some mystical bonds with her children. It's not bad or good. It just exists.

Fathers are replaceable, interchangeable somehow. Perhaps I feel I'm not getting enough from my kids in terms of some magical relationship. I am aware of the difference in the kids' relationship with their mother, but it doesn't frustrate me. I remember in my own family that my own father was distant and quite negative in some respects and my mother was a primary source of comfort. With my own kids, no matter what I do, mother is more there for them.

For Jerry Brumbaugh, fatherhood did not in any major way add to or detract from his sense of who he was—his personal set of strengths and weaknesses, or his basic feeling of competence, which is a key to a satisfactory identity. He did not look to this new life role to provide him with a testing ground for qualities he had not previously been able to exercise concretely. However, if anything, his confidence and competence were incidentally shored up by an affirmative experience with his three young sons.

Others of us choose parenthood partly because we feel our basic strengths are more suited to parenting than the other roles we had tried. As mentioned in the discussion of personal myths, we may even have drawn up a mental checklist of our qualifications for parenthood ahead of time, only to face daily situations that undermined our confidence in those abilities.

Qualities we were certain we possessed are put to a grueling test. We are unquestionably dexterous until we fumble and stab our babies with diaper pins, organized until we find that even going on a short outing becomes a nightmare, flexible until our six-year-old child's dawdling makes her late for school every day, calm under stress until our child falls off the changing table or breaks a leg in a bicycle accident. If we let go of testing our performances as parents, we can even see humor in what some days feels like relentless calamity.

We also look to parenthood as a way of fulfilling parts of ourselves that are not being exercised in our careers. For one woman, the prospect of finally being unchained from a desk and a grinding schedule makes the seemingly unstructured casualness of home life with small children appealing. The spontaneous and playful side of her welcomes an opportunity for fuller expression. While she sometimes finds this need being met as a mother, she also discovers she has let other important needs go.

She discovers she has difficulty structuring her life—or even her child's routine—once cut loose from somebody else's clock. While she does occasionally enjoy playing on the beach and taking long stroller walks, she also finds herself at loose ends without familiar routines. She misses the productive and efficient feeling she derived from working her way through a stack of correspondence before the end of a work day. At this point she can explore new ways to meet her needs for a sense of completion and tangible accomplishment that are not being satisfied in her new role.

So when personal qualities we have wanted to test are tried with uncertain results, or when needs we had hoped to meet are not fulfilled and other ones neglected, we can suffer identity setbacks.

Parenthood can frustrate those of us used to measuring ourselves against objective standards of role performance —in our jobs and schooling—and who are dependent upon this feedback for our identity strength. We may find ourselves acting out this need by reading child development books and comparing our children against the composite children described there, or with the children of friends or relatives. We may measure ourselves against a slick magazine's ideal housewife, or Total Woman, or Wonder Woman, and set ourselves up for failure. We may look to our mates and children for objective feedback they may be unable to give us.

So when we have a need for a report card on our role as a parent and do not get this from our family or peers, we can suffer identity setbacks. And, as discussed earlier, when we find that who we were before we became parents feels threatened we can suffer identity setbacks.

It is somtimes at this point of identity setback that we consider or make big changes in our lives. We turn to other roles: our careers or schooling may assume more importance, or we may give them more of our time. Or we may seek new avocations or relationships that feed other aspects of ourselves than those nourished by parenting. The challenge at this point is to declare a moratorium on drastic role shedding before we have the opportunity to develop our own ability to live with the pleasures of one role while we are learning about it and, in the process, about ourselves.

Caught between our definitions

This particular crisis of identity was once and still seems to be more commonly experienced by mothers. Until a few years ago, motherhood was an exclusive role of long duration. A woman became a parent, and if she was to be a "good" mother, other roles were abandoned or deferred until her mothering role was completed. If a woman felt unsuccessful, incompetent, or incomplete as a parent, she had limited options—either to try harder to meet a perhaps impossible standard of performance or to find acceptable, limited tasks in which she could exercise some unmet identity needs.

Fathers, even those who participated more wholly in child raising than the stereotyped absentee breadwinner, were most likely to attach more importance to success or failure in their career roles. Even if they put in a substantial amount of time as fathers, they were less likely to identify themselves in an occupational sense as parents.

We still find this to be largely true. Even while families are operated on a more democratic basis, with both parents putting in shared time and taking responsibility for child raising, than might have been found ten years ago, women more so than men find themselves profoundly identified with their role as parents.

Fathers tend to express personal change in terms of a loss of the playful and carefree time of their lives, a feeling of assumed responsibility and maturity. Women describe a letting go of what Gail Sheehy in *Passages* has labeled the Seeker Self, the achieving self.

These elements that trigger identity setbacks have been felt by generations of mothers. And increasingly, as parenthood is a clearer choice, we view this role with more responsibility and with a sense of all the "shoulds" and "should nots." We want to be successful parents, and we want also to feel competent in other areas of our lives. The woman at the beginning of this chapter who was "frightened by this emerging freedom of choice" expresses a common reaction to the numbers of role models from which she may choose and the real options she has for her life as a wife and mother.

The new consciousness that gives overdue support for the liberation of women from limited traditional roles may at the same time substitute entrapment in a Super Role. Surrounded by and aware of numerous options for our lives, we may buckle under pressure to act on more than we can handle at one time. We may feel pushed by a prevalent script for the ideal parent into a larger-than-life stance as Wonder Woman—who can do all things at all times—losing much of what we might gain by experiencing fewer roles more fully.

A woman lawyer who left her law practice to take the time to have children began to panic when she was unable to concentrate on reading the newspaper at the end of a day with a prowling, demanding two-year-old who had suddenly stopped napping. She was sure that she would no longer be able to handle her career work load and, more important, to think, when she resumed her practice. So she hired a live-in baby-sitter and returned prematurely to her office. She had wanted to return perhaps part-time to law, just to exercise those faculties she was afraid to lose, but she took the first available option—nine-to-five work— and then felt retrapped and overwhelmed in the life she had wanted to break away from.

Lisa was determined to keep teaching school full-time and simultaneously raise her two small sons. She took only two weeks off before her first son's birth and a week after. She timed her second child's birth for summer vacation break. For four years she was "Super Teach," earth mother, bread baker, and a community political leader. When migraine headaches caused her to take two months' sick leave, she was forced to reevaluate her life plan. She realized she had "tried so hard to be all women, to not be stuck in the housewife rut," that she was afraid to find out what might happen if she let go of any of her other roles. And she was even more afraid she would decide she would rather stay home.

A side effect of our expanded consciousness of other possibilities for our lives as women may be a sense of self-consciousness, even embarrassment, about the role of parent, our nurturing and teaching sides. Instead of being pacesetters for a new age of true freedom of choice of roles and individualized life design, we may find ourselves as constricted as our Victorian ancestors by the dicta of the community around us. We are bombarded by the pronouncements of the mass media, which propagandize for and against having a family at all, or which dictate the role model in vogue. One year they may hold up the working parent as the ideal parent, and then swing back the next season to the stay-at-home mother. No wonder we have difficulty hearing our own inner voices in the shrill din.

We can sometimes sense that there is more support, a disproportionate amount of support, for the fulfillment of other roles than motherhood and fatherhood. We need to shore up within ourselves the conviction that these are vital—yes, critical—roles to be played out in our lifetimes. We need to reach out for support from our peers and from our families for the significance of these roles.

Our full human growth and whole identity will not be diminished by being fulfilled in our parenting roles. Nor will our competence as parents be undermined by exploring other identities. Keeping in touch with who we are and discovering the process of identifying our needs can only strengthen all the relationships within a family.

Interviews

Is the grass really greener?

As the old saying goes, things always seem to be better where we are not. From outside, parenthood can sometimes look more inviting than what we have been doing in our careers. Once we become parents, we may find ourselves longing for the greener pastures back on the other side.

These parents have taken a clear-eyed look at their careers and the role they play in their new identities as parents:

Jody age 34; child, age 4:

If my greatest love was urban renewal, I would have fallen seven steps behind while I was raising Rebecca. I could not possibly find part-time work for a satisfactory agency. I would have felt desperately lost. But that part of my life I felt willing to let go. But for someone else it might have been disastrous.

Kathy, age 26; child, age 2:

I was trained in Switzerland as a lab technician. When I decided to have children I knew I could always go back to work when I felt I should. I wanted to take the time out for raising my children. I translate lab reports to keep in touch with my field and devote most of my time to my child. I feel no sense of loss.

Jane, age 36; two sons, ages 14, 12:

I had the beginnings of a career and it was an exciting one. I knew what my profession was going to be but I also felt a pressure of time. I was twenty-two. I felt an artificial urgency about the whole endeavor [child raising]. I was just beginning to feel part of my field, but at the same time I had a concept of myself as a female. If I didn't have children I would not be a higher being.

Patricia:

When I went back to work only half-time when my daughter was born, people felt I was crazy. Didn't I want more money? I don't care about money. I'm satisfied with being able to live. I really wanted to be at home with her. I didn't quit teaching because I enjoy having that contact with the outside world. I look at work as being a part that affects my life.

Kitty; child, age 6:

When I first became a parent, I left our business which I had been working at seven days a week. We had moved into an apartment before the baby was born and there was no one home in the building all day. It was the first time I ever had so much time on my hands alone and I didn't know what to do with it. I felt left out of the business but I had wanted to have a baby so I didn't mind staying home. Our business is a photography store and I had been taking pictures all day every day. I started to get into seeing photography in a new way from staying home and taking pictures of the baby. I started to explore photography as an art and so when I went back to work one day a week when my baby was sixteen months old, I had gotten into photography in a whole new way.

Brigid, age 29; three children, ages 8, 4, 10 months:
I like my role as a mother. It makes me grow and mature. I am a different person now than I was before I had children, and I like this person more.

Richard, age 35; daughter, age 3:
I know that being a father has made me a better pediatrician. I really appreciate what it's like to have a child who is sick, to be the parent of a child who needs help.

Vickie, age 28; son, age 3:
It's incredible for me to think I can handle both my job [librarian] and parenting. I didn't know if I could do both well. There are other ways that being a parent has made me feel more capable. I really feel capable about things I was not always comfortable doing, like taking care of physical problems, handling injuries. When you are a mother you just do it.

Mica, age 35; three children, ages 8, 6, 7 months:
When my first child was a baby, I was offered a job teaching at a state university but turned it down because I loved being with him so much, and I missed him when I was away from him. I told the person hiring me the reason why I turned the position down, and he probably thought I was crazy. I've never regretted that decision and have allowed my career to play a minor role since I've had children just because that's what feels good to me.

My husband said early on that what we would remember from these years raising our children would be the joy of being with them and not the financial hardships.

Judy, age 34:

I traveled a lot before Christopher came. I felt that I had to keep proving myself. I enjoyed it but I had to do it to be equal or as competent as my friends. They were more outgoing, social. They seemed to be more organized, chic, and had more self-confidence.

When we got pregnant I felt like going to the top of a mountain and shouting, "We did it." I had a friend in La Leche League. I wanted to find out anything because I wanted to be the best mother. I wasn't sure about nursing. My friend encouraged me and I managed to nurse him through her encouragement. My whole self-concept changed. I feel that I'm at least as good a mother as they are. I feel really satisfied with my life. I don't feel I have to travel.

This identity fits me. I was always raised to want to be a mother. None of the other roles fit or satisfied me. I'm real glad that I waited to have a baby. I've done basically what I want to do in the way of traveling and career.

Parenthood: tying up the loose ends

We can stumble into parenthood with foggy notions about how it will enhance our sense of self. We may have decided to have children because we have reached a point in our lives when the other options seem blurred, or because our parents expected us to and we haven't an alternative plan. Our fragile reasons for becoming parents do not necessarily predict our abilities to handle the role. We may just hit on a smashing new identity, or one that will at least help us to feel confident enough about ourselves to build on our success as parents for future roles.

Meg, age 34; daughter, age 7:

I always wanted a kid. I was following a script my parents gave me. My sister was the intellectual one in our family—the one who would have a career. I was the domestic one, the sweet one. I went to college, but I didn't take it seriously. I knew I was going to finish and have a family. I realize now that I got pregnant out of a sense of loose ends in my life, and when it ended, there I still was. I still wasn't clear on who I was and where I was going.

The "secret" of parenting

Our children's behavior can be part of our whole identity package. When they misbehave it lowers our self-esteem.

Anne, age 34; two boys, ages 9, 8:

I think that when I was growing up my parents had a fantasy of me as a responsible adult who would have a college degree and be married. By the time I was twenty-two that is precisely what I had become. But neither they nor I had thought much beyond that point, and when I was at the beginning of my adult life I was at the end of the fantasies, both my own and those held for me. I was stunned by the void I felt, by the total lack of images of what lay beyond that point, and my life suddenly seemed empty and directionless. Because the expectations I had for my own life had been based so largely on those of my parents, I realized that it is important for me to look more closely at what I want for my children, and to be sure that it is neither too grandiose nor too limited.

While I had always assumed that I would have children, I had never given it much thought. Without my realizing it, I had strongly rooted assumptions which colored all my reactions to my children's actual behavior. I believed that the process of raising children would not demand much more attention than I cared to give it but that I would be totally responsible for the "outcome" of my children's development. These assumptions meant that when my children misbehaved, I felt that I was a failure as a mother and also that there was obviously something missing in my "maternal instinct" since I was having to spend so much more time, thought, and energy on the children than I had ever imagined I would or than other parents seemed to. I believed that perhaps there was some secret, some "right way" to raise children and that I had only to tap into it to be assured that I would do a good job. But when I continued to guess my way through each new stage with no certainty that I was doing it "right," I felt insecure and frustrated that others seemed to have the secret but that for some reason I didn't. I also had a tendency to assume that the children should already know what to do in any given situation and so when they didn't, my reaction was one of irritation, as if they had purposely done something to annoy me. Additionally, when they would do any of the testy little things children do, like shoving their spaghetti into their mouths with their hands and then giggling like crazy at the mess, I would immediately have a picture of them as uncouth adults, shunned by those more civilized than they, and then I'd react to the childish act with more force than necessary, reacting more to the future picture than to the action itself.

One of the things that becomes increasingly clear is how closely my fantasies about my children are tied to my own needs or fears. I know, for instance, that one of my weaknesses is caring too much about what other people think of me. This is naturally extended to what other people think of my children. If what I am really concerned about is some kind of acceptance or approval of me, then I tend to try to control my children's behavior to be sure it will lend itself to such approval. Breaking out of this kind of pattern has taken lots of work. I have tried to see my children not as channels for either my fears or my visions of grandeur but rather as unique individuals who have their own paths in life. Seeing the incredibly individual stamp that each of the children has and having some of their very real talents pointed out at an early age helped me to see them as separate people rather than simply as "my children." I have used the information and insights gained to look more closely at their budding skills and to try aligning my efforts more closely with who they naturally are.

Rebelling against motherhood

If we become anxious about being "stuck" in the motherhood role, worried that we are missing out on some critical opportunity to expand our identity, the worrying can literally wear us out. At this point we might take a close look at what we feel we are missing, and the immediate consequences of nervous role trying.

Pamela:
There's always been a pull. For five minutes I would want to be with him, the next five minutes not. I would be in a rut, more tired than I needed to be. I guess I was rebelling against "motherhood" from the start. I didn't want people to think I was a mother like everyone else. Sometimes I could relax, not having to say, "I'm not home for good, I'm going to get a job." My need was to go away for an afternoon and

do something more. I would try to schedule small chunks of time to myself. I couldn't do anything total—leave my child full-time.

I feel like I have some responsibility to stay with him. My husband doesn't feel that way. It's not a gut feeling; it's a head trip with me. When I'm away from them, I don't miss them.

I feel I'm an imaginative parent and a creative one. I feel I'm patient and try to tune in to what he's saying or feeling. I'm not overly pushy or overly anxious. I try to be flexible. I am, however, vaguely dissatisfied with my life in general. He may not know if I'm doing something because I want to, or because I feel I have to.

The fathering role

More attention has been paid to the positive qualities of mothering than to the distinct and positive qualities of fathering. Pat, who is thirty-one and has two children, entered parenthood with a firm grip on the assets he was bringing into his new role and the qualities he hoped to nurture in his children.

Pat:

I had no clear picture of what kind of father I would be. I had been around lots of kids as a teacher—not little babies, but other kids of all ages—and I liked them. I didn't look back at my father and say that's what I would or would not be because my father was already fifty years old when I was born. How could I compare myself as a father at twenty-seven with my own father, who had been so much older?

I thought I had enthusiasm and patience to bring into my role. I wanted to bring in a sense of discipline and a feeling for what I would support in my

children's activities. I wanted my own children because as a parent (versus just teaching children) you
have a greater stake, more commitment. I wanted my
own child as an issue of me, seeing myself as a man
and a father.

I wanted a son the first time because I had grown
up around more males and felt more comfortable
about them. I was in school and was home the first
months. I saw the responsibilities and pressures that
my wife faced and I had them also. I didn't feel the
real depressions she had, but did feel a lack of energy
from the night feedings and strange hours. She had
tried to breast-feed and couldn't, and that was very
hard for her to give up. When Mathew went on a
bottle, it was a matter of taking turns—one after the
other. And there were always new challenges—when
he was sick, what do we do about his runny nose or
his runny bowels or his diaper rash?

I never felt in any sense diminished by these challenges and when I felt at a loss I never felt that my
competence as a person in general was threatened.
The new identity I felt was very positive: I had a
child. I was a father—and all that means in terms of
masculinity and sexuality. I wasn't sterile—that's what
it proved on the simplest level.

I found in myself a sense of patience and understanding of the different stages that children pass
through. I sometimes was frustrated and angered by
these stages, but when I could distance myself I
was in awe of these processes that they go through
in their growing.

I'm a different person now than I was at twenty-
seven. I'm a different parent. The other world I live
in is my professional world. There I find relatively
few people who have children, and I have found
increasingly that our value systems and interests are
different. One's role is different as a parent, what

you do with your time and how you conduct yourself. For me it's harder to relate to men who are not parents. Parenting has changed me. It's hard to separate what changes are coming from a difference in age and changes in profession and what parenting has taught me.

As a parent I would like to see them grow into alive, vital, curious adults, interested in what's around them, not buffaloed into things without thought—independent. I feel as a father I can promote a sense of searching, a pride of accomplishment. I can give them chances to work through their frustrations, and a sense of direction—what is appropriate and inappropriate in what they do. I don't feel a basic difference in my role and my wife's role—we bring different things to our children because we are different people.

House fathering

This father experienced a feeling of loss and isolation similar to that felt by women who find themselves suddenly cut off from old identities and old companions in other jobs when they are home all day with small children. He experienced also a sense of alienation from his mate similar to one many women have expressed. She was out in the world doing what he assumed were interesting things and meeting interesting people. And there he was at home.

Jim:

Sarah Elena, our first child, was born in England, and I recall the time as being full of excitement, love, joy. I was feeling at a peak of personal power; my marriage seemed totally secure, I felt as though I

was on the edge of a spectacular professional success, and altogether life seemed emminently livable.
Well, some crashing, shattering failures, full of misery
and boringly predictable depressions, were waiting
not far down the road. But for that first year of Sarah
Elena's life I felt great. I had a brief time—how long
actually I cannot say, but I remember it as lasting for
two months—where I was disappointed that our first
child was not a boy. I wanted a son for all the reasons
men want sons; some of them chauvinistic, others
simply because the male in me easily identifies with
maleness and I like men and boys; hence, I wanted
a son.

For the first year after Sarah was born Dori and I
lived together in Greece and Germany. We shared
chores in both places and I did not feel cramped,
short of space or time. I was not working at a job
then. I wrote each day but never for more than six
hours, usually for four or five. I felt that our lives
were quite well balanced. Neither of us carrying too
much of a burden. This was while we were in Greece
and Sarah was growing from a newborn to a nine-
month-old beauty. We needed money, as others have
needed it before us, and our stay in Greece, which
was idyllic, ended on a very sour note. for me. We
were broke, something that did not particularly worry
me. The real pain for me came when we were about
to leave for Germany and I learned that my novel
had been rejected by an English publisher who had
promised to publish it. So off to Germany we went,
where Dori began working, teaching at an American
school, and I settled into a life of house father.

House fathering was very boring. I had all the
complaints every house person suffers but my case
was unique. I was in a small Bavarian village and
other house people did not accept males into their

midst. I was never invited to the kaffee klatsches the women playing my role enjoyed, and I was thereby denied the safety valve that women have when they group together and complain about the dullness of their lot. It was during this time that I began to resent doing "all" the shopping, "all" the driving to and fro, "all" the this, and "all" the that. What had happened, I can now see, is that the balance Dori and I knew in Greece had been broken. She had become totally responsible for our finances. I was fully responsible for our domestic life. We shared little except the same space and liked what we were doing less and less.

Aaron Joseph was born during a downward spiral for me. I did not know what exactly was wrong but I suspect now that, as much as anything else, it was the fact that our lives were so unbalanced. This disharmony continued through Sarah's second year and Aaron's first. It went on after we returned to the States and is still something we have to deal with. And what it amounts to, I think, is an alienation. An inability for either Dori or me to know what the other is doing. I do not think the problems that have come about following Sarah's and Aaron's births are because of them. They are, I think, the result of working at nine-to-five jobs, trying to live as a nuclear family with very little support from the community we live in, and not knowing what my wife and children do all day; and also, not being able to share my working life (which is more than a third of my conscious life) with them.

Untangling our identities

Our identities and our hopes for our children tend to become intertwined. If we can be honest enough to admit that some of our children's shortcomings—as we see them—reflect our feelings about ourselves, we have taken an important step toward seeing our children as they are.

Jerry, age 30; two children, ages 4, 2:

Q.: How do you feel you've changed since you've had children?

A.: I've been conscious of needing to be more directed, more settled. I have felt more insecure; all of a sudden you're supposed to be capable—you're a father—and nothing has really changed except you've had these children, and you're supposed to be competent.

Q.: Have you experienced a positive sense of change?

A.: Since our children are so beautiful and seem to be bright and interesting I feel good sometimes about myself. If they are developing well, you've something to feel good about in yourself. Before I had children I had the sense that I was what I was —with the limits already there. Then you have children who are, genetically at least, fifty percent yours, and you wonder what's going to happen to them—and to you, since they are a part of you. . . . I also worry about them being like me—all those negative parts of me. With our son, I worry he's not physical enough because I wasn't very physical, or shy because I'm shy.

Everything that's positive I feel I see coming from my wife. I worry a lot about all the negative qualities I might have brought my children. I worry more about my son, not because he is male, but because he is our firstborn. You can't go back on those things you do with your first. The second, you do change somehow. . . . I have decided just to concentrate on cuddling my daughter and not be so concerned about doing things with her—and then worrying about whether we've done enough or too little or the right things.

A cultural identity

Our identity also reflects our cultural framework. For the person with two cultures to choose from, there are two roads to walk on for gaining a sense of self.

Linda Locklear-Mojel is a Native American. She is thirty, has a one-year-old child, and works as a counselor and teacher of Native American studies. She thinks the identity crisis is an Anglo phenomenon.

Linda:

Here I am thirty years old and have a one-year-old daughter. In non-Indian society that's looked upon as old to have a child. You're over the hill.

In white society, being thirty and a woman is not a good thing. In the Indian world growing older is a neat thing. The older you are the more power, responsibility, and knowledge you have. Getting gray hair is a good sign, a sign that you've finally learned something.

I feel like I'm a marginal person. I'm walking on two roads at the same time. I'm better if I can keep my feet on two roads. If I get too much on one side I have trouble in the white world. I have a built-in check and balance and I think it makes me more sensitive to what's going on.

If I were just white, turning thirty and becoming a mother would have been a crisis. If I were just Indian I wouldn't have noticed, it would have been just part of the life process. That's how we look at life. The Indian wedding ceremony is a circle. Life is a circle. Somebody dies. Somebody else gets born. Somebody else gets married.

My identity crisis of turning thirty was resolved when I spoke in a class on Indian aging. It put me back in touch with my Indian self—my real feelings about aging.

I feel like our baby has joined us in our life process. In the dominant culture they make such a big deal about everything. They tell you when you have a child it will change your life and so it does. It's a self-fulfilling prophecy. I experienced things after her birth but I accepted them. I do better on my own than reading things. There's no preparation but experience. The more acculturated Indian women have more of a problem. I'm in the white culture but I'm also more sensitive to the old. It gives you something.

We Indians have an identity problem to begin with, having lost our culture, not being in the mainstream culture. Therefore you don't have all the little identity crises. *The dominant culture is crisis oriented.* They don't relate to the positive processes of life. They create problems. It fulfills one of their needs.

We want Ushla to learn her native language. We think it's important for her to have a feeling for what it is to be Indian. We want her to have a choice, to be able to have an Indian identity. Then if she doesn't want to, that's fine.

What do you enjoy about parenting?

Giora, age 40; three children, ages 7, 4, 2:

I enjoy the authority. Being in charge. It's a challenge. God put these little creatures in my charge and it's a challenge to see if I can make something out of them. To make a balance between not doing too much for them and not neglecting them. The whole game is interesting.

Marta, age 29; two children, ages 8, 7:

I suppose the thing I enjoy the most about being a mother is having two children, two human beings that I can love as much as they love me. It's already there, the love, it's automatic. No matter how hard it gets the love is always there. It's kind of nice to have someone whose life you can form in a certain way. What I like most though is that we all love each other.

Sandra, age 40; three children, ages 19, 17, 14:

It's fun. The communication. It keeps you young and with young thoughts. Especially when they're teen-agers discovering their own identities it's fun to see what's happening to them. What I find interesting now is to see them breaking away from home. My neighbor's children are younger and they're so afraid of them leaving, of growing up and going to college and moving out. But I think it's exciting. I feel like I'm looking forward instead of back.

Brigid, age 29; three children, ages 8, 4, 10 months:

I enjoy the purity and beauty of my children, the inner beauty. When I think of my children I feel rich.

Ira, age 41; two children, ages 9, 7:

I enjoy:
The love it spontaneously elicits,
The challenge,
The inevitably consequent humility.

Anne, age 34; two children, ages 9, 8:

Parenting has probably been the impetus for more personal growth than anything in my life.

Carol, age 44; seven children, ages 24, 21, 18, 17, 15, 13, 11:

When I first had them I loved creating something so perfect as small babies. I couldn't get enough of them. I love watching them grow. Probably the best part is seeing them become independent humans. It seems like yesterday they were babies. One of my children is a parent now and I've loved seeing some of my values reflected in his parenting. Someone asked recently who my best friends are—who I like to go places with—and I realized of all people I prefer spending time with my children. On the one hand I'm so thrilled when one of them moves out, it's like I've made it seeing them independent, but on the other hand I love being with them. And they said that on Thanksgiving there's no place else they would want to go. I always had a baby around to fulfill my love for babies but I never realized that the biggest reward came later on. People complain about teenagers but I think they're great. I remember being idealistic like they are.

My husband was very nonplussed about having kids. He came from a hard situation but he's become a high school teacher. One thing he said that was very important was never take what a teenager says personally. I remember saying my father was vain because I wanted to use the bathroom mirror. When my mother told me he was hurt for two weeks I couldn't believe it. I didn't mean it; I just wanted to use the mirror.

Because of my experiences as a parent I have much faith that I can do a good job with parenting. I get upset with the idea of doing things in one way or from the book. I think people get confused by books. I feel they have their own innate feeling of how to parent.

NOTES

1. Enid Rubin, "Some Thoughts on Marriage," "California Living" section, *San Francisco Examiner*, December 26, 1976, p. 22.
2. William Glasser, *The Identity Society* (New York: Harper & Row, 1972), p. 8.
3. Erik Erikson, *Identity: Youth and Crisis* (New York: W. W. Norton & Co., 1968), p. 138.
4. *Ibid.*, p. 132.
5. Edward H. Pohlman, *Psychology of Birth Planning* (Cambridge, Mass.: Schenkman Publishing Co., 1969), pp. 35–81. (Summary of reasons for wanting children)
6. Gail Sheehy, *Passages*, p. 70.
7. Maureen Green, *Fathering* (New York: McGraw-Hill, 1977), p. 20.

5. Balancing Needs

"No one ever told me I would be up at night,
and that I would be exhausted."

—A parent

"I never knew I could love or be loved
so unconditionally."

—A parent

With so many books on the care of children, why are there none about the care and feeding of a parent's needs? We have endless books and articles that inform us about the primacy of our children's needs and how we can best serve them. They instruct us about the importance of changing our behavior and even our life-styles where our children's most basic needs are concerned. The experts constantly remind us of our critical role as the reservoir from which our children's sense of physical and emotional well-being must be continually filled.

Yet it is only in recent years that the matter of parents' needs has even been an issue. That issue has grown out of the unresolved controversy over whether or not a mother should work. Many people see this as a needs issue, rather than a strictly financial one, the premise being that if a woman stays home, she is denying her own need for achievement, and if she works, she is endangering her child's need for a sense of security.

Unfortunately, the arguments on both sides, no matter how valid, form a very simplistic approach to looking at the whole process of balancing our needs, as we will discuss later. Nevertheless, the lively debate on this subject has served an important function in bringing the concept of parental growth and development into the popular consciousness. But it is a rather lonely bulwark for the discussion of parents' needs. Even in the wave of adult self-exploration that has been sweeping our society, the subject of parents and their needs has been conspicuously overlooked.

It is true that in some of the literature on being "good" parents there is an occasional reference to the importance of parents' remembering to nurture and pay attention to themselves. There are admonitions to "be sure and take time for yourself" and to "have fun as a couple" or general admonitions about the danger of ignoring your own needs (often because that is bad for the child). But these occasional prescriptions do not begin to equip us for the challenging process of understanding and sorting out our needs as parents. Looking at and balancing needs is a process; these pieces of advice are like the techniques offered for raising children. They don't work as tools unless they grow out of our understanding of our children and ourselves.

One of the basic problems is that even before we are parents we tend to look at needs, at least psychological ones, in too limited a way. At an early age we learn specific ways of fulfilling needs for recognition, for attention, and for power. These often work quite well for us, the major problem being that once we become adapted to them it is often hard to give them up. As children, we may create a scene to receive attention. Instead of expanding our ways of receiving attention as we grow older, we may continue to cling to that pattern even into adulthood. A more productive tack would be to try out new avenues to fulfillment as they present themselves, accepting or rejecting them according to their usefulness in a given situation.

Another aspect of this problem of seeing our needs in narrow ways is that we learn to put a lot of energy into areas where we can meet our needs easily and neglect areas where attendance to our needs would cost us more effort. A shy adolescent boy may have channeled his needs for being assertive or even aggressive with people into academic achievement, if it comes easily to him. As he grows older, the process of branching out and meeting his needs for intimacy and even aggression should flow from his natural growth as an adult. But what most often happens is that his needs remain somewhat unbalanced unless he learns how to divert some of the energy he has put into achievement into other needier areas of his life.

The subject of needs is both a simple and a complex one. We know unconsciously how to fill most of our needs without having to think about them. It is usually only when we are changing or our life situation is demanding that we change that we must be aware of our needs, let alone explore new ways of meeting them. Parenthood makes these kinds of demands. We enter into parenthood, first of all, with the idea that it will fill some new and neglected needs. We also expect that our new role will offer us not only a new identity but an expanded picture of our whole sense of self.

People who are actively engaged in trying to understand their own growth and the ways parenthood might influence it could benefit from focusing on at least four related tasks:

1. looking at their patterns for filling needs before they were parents;

2. becoming aware of the way their identities as parents affect their view of their own needs and the process of fulfilling them;

3. expanding their vision of what their needs are and finding more creative ways of looking at them;

4. seeing the balancing of needs with those of other family members as a continuing opportunity, rather than a series of arbitrary decisions.

Why our old patterns are important

If we look at needs as plants growing in a garden, we will find some tenderly nurtured, perhaps even oversized from our constant cultivation; others might be starved for fertilizer and choked by weeds. If we have the view that we are, even within ourselves, always seeking a balance, this image can be an important one. Like that adolescent who fills many of his needs through the route of academic achievement, we all tend to put high energy into the areas of our life that have given us satisfaction and ignore or put much less energy into areas that don't give us back enough.

Parenthood comes into the picture by giving us the opportunity (or if we resist, by demanding) that we look at our neglected areas. In fact, as mentioned previously, most of us enter parenthood with the expectation that it will help us to attend to our neglected needs or parts of ourselves, the unweeded areas. In the chapter on personal myths, we could see that people's reasons for becoming parents have little to do with the actual enjoyment of children. They are almost all concerned with the needs for nurturance, either given or received, or the development of an expanded identity.

Of course, as shown, our pictures of how this will happen are often quite unrealistic, just because we cannot predict experience ahead of time. But in choosing parenthood for any of these reasons, we are opting for growth, even if we cannot know what form this growth will take.

One father uses his own experience of the last eight years as an example. Having been a student until the age of twenty-six, he saw parenthood as an opportunity to work on his neglected needs for responsibility and effectiveness in the real world. His fantasy about parenthood was that having a child would provide him with such motivation for aggression and responsibility that he would enjoy new areas of success in the world.

The problem came when parenting demanded too abrupt a change in his ability to focus on those neglected needs. He wasn't entirely aware that his years of schooling had been in a sense a haven that kept him from having to assume more responsibility. His view of parenthood was in many ways realistic. It did motivate him toward greater responsibility, but the change was a difficult one, and the skills and satisfaction in making the shift did not come automatically.

However, parenthood did provide him with real joys in meeting his needs for intimacy and nurturance: "I reveled in being able to express affection in such totally uninhibited ways. I took on a new identity, the liberated person. I helped with every aspect of the baby. I felt really proud of that."

This extremely satisfactory expansion of needs and sense of himself helped offset the trials of having to become adjusted to new parts of himself in the world. However, the knowledge that he was working on a part of himself that he had chosen—qualities that he wanted to develop and needs he chose to meet—made the transition bearable. If he had been forced into becoming responsible, or had not seen it as a quality that he wanted to develop, entering parenthood might have precipitated a crisis.

As we discussed in Chapter 2, looking at our fantasies can give us a glimpse of how we feel our needs would be met by parenthood. In Harold's myth we see the expression of high needs for autonomy, along with his expectation that becoming a father would fill some unmet needs for security and admiration.

One man who is already a parent saw autonomy as one of his highest needs before having children. He was a dedicated outdoorsman:

Before I was married I could not have gone a week without getting out in the country and spending some time alone. I really felt that I could not exist without spending a lot of time outdoors. The demands of parenthood shocked me at first. I had almost no time for walks, let alone rock climbing. It was a question of priorities; there was so much to be done and I wanted to be a good father. It was not hard. But I began to see that I could meet those needs in other ways. Now, as my children are getting older, I have begun to get in the outdoors more with them. But I don't see it as absolutely essential, the way I did before.

Once we get even a sketchy picture of how we have defined our needs and how they have defined us, we can pay attention to using parenthood as an opportunity to enlarge our options in the ways all our needs can be met. We can let our new identity as a parent strengthen aspects of ourselves that have been previously neglected.

Our identities are so connected with the way we have learned to accommodate our needs that it would be hard and perhaps pointless to decide which was the cause and which the effect; they are in fact quite interdependent.

One example of this intertwining of identity and needs is the stereotype of the man with a "macho" identity. His high needs (as he might consciously express them) would include autonomy, a need for dominance and aggression and possibly for achievement. His low needs as he sees them might be for intimacy, for nurturance and the nurturance of others.

We can see from the sketch of this personality that it would be hard to define whether the "macho" identity had determined his needs or whether it was the reverse. This points to the importance of being aware that our attendance to certain needs is crucial to our sense of who we are and what we want to be.

Parenthood enlarges our picture by calling on us to reevaluate our old patterns of fulfillment, some of which (achievement or autonomy, for instance) may have been crucial to our preparenthood identity. But, as discussed in the previous chapter, parenthood also introduces an identity of its own, with needs and qualities that we feel are important to our sense of well-being in this new role.

This expansion of our identity is usually more rewarding. Again, it only calls up our capacities for growth when the needs of our old identity conflict with the needs of the new one.

An artist who is the divorced mother of two girls, ages ten and six, had always seen herself as a spontaneous, expressive person who took delight in her inconsistencies. Going through a divorce has caused her to work with specific needs in her daughters. She has consciously had to develop new qualities in the part of her involved with being a parent:

One of my daughters is very concerned that I be a mother like "other mothers." To her, this means staying home, baking cookies, and having a very predictable life. She doesn't like big changes in life-style—something that had excited me—or to move around a lot. I tell her that in some ways I am like those other mothers. We do bake cookies. I also go out on dates. I have tried, when possible, to structure a very regular routine for my children with consistent ways of handling them. My ex-husband is so immature. He is very inconsistent with them. One night they will stay up until midnight, and the next he'll send them to bed at six. I have learned to accommodate their needs for predictability and security. The divorce has put them through so much. I feel good about knowing that I can meet their needs at this time.

These are choices that this parent has made. They have grown out of her perceptions of what is important in a specific period of parenthood. She did not decide when her children were born that she would change her life-style and give up some of its spontaneity. It is her ability to keep a fluid identity and to assess the individual needs of the situation that gives her the ability to handle her two identities creatively.

There will be inevitable conflicts between our old identity and our images of ourselves as a parent. The person who loves parties has different needs than does the parent who wants a stable home environment. The achiever or community organizer can have different needs from those of a person who wants to spend the bulk of his time with his children. The mate has conflicts with the needs of the parent. Being a parent does not imply having just one identity—or filling one need. There will be conflicts within these identities as parents: the nurturer versus the disciplinarian, the model versus the real person. It is only when we meet these tensions arbitrarily, choosing the either/or solution, that everyone's needs for growth are bound to suffer.

Meeting our needs

In Chapter 4 we discussed some pros and cons of having a child either earlier or later in our own development. In discussing needs, we can see again that the particular point at which we choose to have our first or later children affects us each individually, depending on our values, goals, and needs. A young person may not have (as mentioned previously) a fixed identity or needs that are rigidly tied to it. But a person who has a child at a later point in life may have filled certain high needs and established a clear identity, making her more willing to postpone or see how her needs can be filled in new ways.

One mother who had spent many years in school and working before she had her baby said: "There is nothing like it [motherhood] for intimacy, especially when you're nursing. I can enjoy just being with the baby and nurturing her growth, instead of needing to perform in the world. That's very satisfying for me right now." This mother also worked at expanding ways of filling old needs. For years she had wanted to pursue an interest in dance but had never had time. She has begun taking dance three times a week and feels she is meeting a long-postponed goal.

If our ideal parent is too prescriptive, her rules can keep

us from meeting our needs creatively. Both the woman
who feels her child's needs have to come first and the
woman who feels she has to balance children, home, and
job without outside help are in the grip of mistaken certainties. One of the most prevalent mistaken certainties
that parents have about needs is the philosophy of the
either/or. Either I put myself first or I defer my needs for
my child. Either I let my children be independent and
spontaneous or I set limits for them. This either/or approach is an especially shallow one when it is applied to
our needs; it is actually the continual balancing of our
needs with those of the people around us that helps us to
grow. The woman who decides to go back to work after
her baby is a few months old, not because finances dictate
it but because she is convinced that she is denying her
own needs, may be denying herself some of the growth
she wanted from parenthood. We tend to look at a situation like this as either right or wrong. The point is that
when we are in the process of exploring new needs and
areas of ourselves it is important to give ourselves time, to
avoid the trap of the either/or.

Balancing our needs with the needs of others

Our myths of parenting, as noted at the beginning of this
chapter, will quite often predetermine the amount and
kind of attention we think we should give to nurturing
our children and/or nurturing ourselves. We hope that
delicate juxtaposition will grow and change at the many
points of parenthood when our pictures no longer fit what
we or others need. In the beginning we have to juggle
even our physical needs, and meeting them can be our
highest priority.

The simple fixed needs for adequate rest, regular mealtimes, and periods of relaxation had been satisfied for so

long before we became parents that we were unaware of their critical effect on our well-being and control. Even though we might have been told that the needs of an infant would upset our routines, we were certainly not fully prepared for the devastating effect that denial or deferral of these needs could have on us over a period of weeks or months. If our baby does not, as predicted, stay asleep all night by the age of three months, the need for rest and, maybe more important, the need for a semblance of *what was before the baby* can be a gnawing pain.

Refreshed by the newness and wonder of our baby, we may run on exhilarated energy, undiminished by rest and relaxation—for a time. Eventually we may become depressed by the complex of hormones and emotions labeled postpartum "baby blues," and our need for sleep and solitude may be suddenly acute. Then it can take an emotional crisis to understand with clarity exactly what we have been lacking.

This is often the first point at which a mother realizes that she can become so caught up in the conscientious and well-meaning fulfillment of her child's needs that she woefully neglects her own. Once she takes inventory, she can find rather simple ways of attending to herself. She can use the baby's nap times as a quiet nurturing period for her—not as a time for frantic housecleaning. She can begin to look at her standards of performance as a cook, cleaner, and mother. Can she let go of expectations that may end up leaving her discouraged and exhausted?

Especially for new parents, the increased demands on their time and energies can intensify the needs of both for nurturance. First-time fathers often comment on how much more responsible they suddenly feel. At the same time they are taking on a heavier practical and emotional load, their increased need for comfort and empathy from their wives is not being met. The balancing act often involves more than a parent and a child; it frequently involves weighing the needs of both parents and their children. Sensitivity to imbalances in the fulfillment of needs is crucial to the restoration of balance and harmony.

Life with a toddler

The placid baby who was a charming addition to the evening meal becomes a demanding and distracting toddler and prompts a reexamination of his mother's needs. One woman told us:

> One night we had guests who had come five hundred miles to visit with us. I spent the entire meal preparing Jamie's food, teasing him into sitting in his high chair and eating his vegetables, picking up his thrown food, and answering his patter. . . . I was so much into this nightly routine that the fact that I was ignoring our guests, not even sitting with them, didn't enter my mind. I was doing for Jamie. My husband was furious after they left. When we both calmed down, we talked about how we needed to have a meal—even just by ourselves—that didn't center around an eighteen-month-old child.

This mother was operating out of a strong conviction that children should be included in all of their parents' activities at home, and that any other arrangement would cause her son long-term distress. This belief prevented her from observing that an active—and testy—toddler may not be ready to be included at those meals where adult needs for quiet conversation and leisurely eating must also be satisfied.

The confrontation with her husband over the chaotic dinner with guests caused her to rethink how the needs of her child and of the adults in the family could be met. She began to give earlier meals to her son, spending necessary time with him without feeling overly obligated. Then she, her husband, and guests could have a more relaxed time together. She could begin to reestablish a place for herself in what she calls "the world of grown-ups."

Facing a similar situation, we can work out this and

other problems in a variety of ways. For example, we might feel comfortable letting go of that adult social time and entertaining, or we might concentrate on being less concerned about mealtimes as a social experience for the baby. Solutions to this type of family problem depend on honest discussion and evaluation of conflicting needs.

For this couple, meals had always served as an intimate sharing time. He worked long and often erratic hours in his business, and the evening meal was one of their few dependable times together. She had, first out of willingness and then out of a sense of duty, relinquished this pleasurable part of their routine when the baby arrived. While she enjoyed creating a congenial mealtime for her young son, she also saw the need to balance her involvements and responsibilities as an adult and mate with her feelings of devotion and responsibility toward her child.

Changing needs

Some parents protest that they do not acutely feel their needs and their children's as separate, perhaps because of their satisfaction in being able to serve each other. But children change and grow, and one day they will no longer need the same things we had been giving them. So even if our own accommodations of our children's needs work for months or even years, there will be times of crisis when all members of a family must look at each other and themselves in new ways.

There may come a time when your teenage girl exchanges her intimacy and sharing with you for widening involvement with peers. You may feel this necessary moving away as an aching loss and raw need. You may have ritually complained about the chore of fixing your child's lunch until your child announces, "Don't fix it for me. I'm old enough to make my own." These acts of sharing and doing fulfill parents' needs to serve and accommodate. But it is not just our own changing needs that cause us to chafe against others in our family. Our children who fulfill some of our needs change in their accustomed roles, thus causing tension.

The mother of a fifteen-year-old son who had dropped out of school discovered some of her hidden needs as a side result of family crisis. While undergoing group counseling with her family, she became interested in individual help.

She had always felt poor in comparison to her ideal parent, who was "always loving and kind to her children." When her son was in crisis, she called up all the best resources she had as a parent to help him through, and still she was unable to solve his problems for him.

"It was proof to me that I had to be detached," she said. She found that when she no longer expected to fulfill his needs or prevent his mistakes, she could allow him both anger toward and reliance on her.

` Letting go of those dictates from the ideal parent enabled her to start sorting out her needs as a person from those of her family. It was not an easy transition; while she had been willing to spend time and money on family therapy, she had strong reservations about spending the time, money, and attention on herself. Her decision to enter into individual counseling was the crucial step in embracing her own needs. With the support of her therapist, she rediscovered ways of nurturing herself. She found time to be alone, to come in contact with nature on walks and in her garden, and to touch base with her feelings.

Before marriage she had sometimes stormed out of the house and had taken solitary walks: "That was a different experience. I had always left in desperation. I felt I was running away from home. Now I can feel single. It's a feeling of inner freedom to take care of my needs, and to have friends and relationships outside my family."

What sparks the periodic reevaluation of needs and priorities? It can be a sudden side effect of crises: illness, death, divorce, or an abusive loss of control. For other parents, this recognition and resolution happens more gradually and runs a smoother course. For still others, the disequilibrium symptomatic of a period of changing needs may be denied, buried, or misnamed.

Denying or avoiding a period of changing needs can perhaps cause the most pain. Our needs are left, shadowy and ill-defined, on the back burner of our daily routine, and our ignorance of them can leave us open to periods of great confusion, anxiety, or even potential explosion.

The parent who talked about her explosive shadow parent in the chapter on personal myths and fantasies began to break from a destructive pattern of relationships with her children when she saw clearly where her ideal parent left off and her real needs and abilities began. She is now in the process of finding a role more relaxed than the stern expectations of her ideal parent and a realistic balancing of her needs with those of her three young children.

It is learning to pinpoint and to balance our needs and those of our family that can lead us toward the greatest harmony and satisfaction within ourselves. As one parent said, "I feel like a person now instead of a mother. Discovering my needs has been a process of unveiling, rather than changing who I am."

Interviews

Needs

Mary, age 30; two daughters, ages 6, 3:

I always have felt I needed time in the evening when I didn't do anything for my children. It took me a long time to split, to separate out my needs—reading, writing, and thinking—and as my children grew, my needs also expanded to a need for more outside time. I asked Tom to help more. I took them with me to see friends. I expected them to adjust to my needs. It didn't always work. Once we tried to go to a drive-in movie when Emily was fourteen months old. I spent the whole time walking up and down the rows of cars.

Kathleen, single mother; child, age 2:

In the early weeks my mother did everything but nurse the baby, so things went pretty well. The first time I began to be tied down was when I was in a small house in Minnesota in the middle of winter. Sean was eighteen months old. He was no longer taking two naps. He wasn't responding to discipline when I said no, and I didn't know what else to do.

I began taking classes, a toddler class at the local Y, a parenting class at an adult school. I learned to try to communicate with him past just "No," and that made me feel more successful. But I wasn't getting much time away from him.

One thing the others in my parents class suggested to me was that I let him help me do some small things around the house, like the dishes. I didn't know much about children before, what they really were capable of performing.

I started to go out to work a little, so I had a little more time to myself. When spring came and we could be outside, it helped.

Karen:

As he got older, his dependency was hard for me. When he was nine months old, I remember I was trying to can some fruit, and he insisted on riding on my back the whole time. I respected who he was always, but I didn't always like it. When I made choices between my needs and his, he won—most of the time. There were a few things he had no choice about—he was left with baby-sitters whether he liked it or not.

Making compromises

When we begin to compare and evaluate our needs and those of our family, the resolution is rarely one-sided. Neither the parent's nor the child's needs consistently win out. We make compromises all the way along; different periods in our relationships will bring shifts in the balance.

Reggie, who is thirty-five and has a four-year-old daughter, decided to defer her return to work in order to attend to what she felt were her daughter's special needs for guidance and nurturance. The fact that she was clear about her reasons for choosing to stay home will make her decision a more comfortable one.

Q.: Have you ever had to define your own needs in terms of your daughter's?

Reggie:

Yes, I suppose I have. I kept postponing going back to teaching, even though we could use the money, and I sometimes feel like I should be doing other things, because I felt she needed me. This spring, my last chance to go back ran out. I still think she needs me more than I need to go back to teaching. I need to be there for her, to keep her in line—she is so willful and can be difficult, I know. Also to take her where she needs to go. I want to do that for her.

Q.: Have there been times when you have had to define your needs in terms of your child's?

Kathleen:

In terms of needs, he usually wins. Children are more persistent. We learn to delay gratification. I try to be clear when I really need more quiet, more sleep. My move to Berkeley was meeting my need to be back here, not his need. He is missing his extended natural family. We're moving out of a house with a roommate into our own place out of my need. It is good for him to be around other adults, and she has two children, but I feel uncomfortable. I feel she is too permissive and inconsistent with her children, and they're manipulative as a result.

Making a decision about moving is a common balancing act. This mother had to choose between staying near her parents, so that her son could enjoy an extended family, and her own need to make a life of her own. Her second decision to leave a communal household for an apartment also meant weighing her son's enjoyment of surrogate siblings against her unhappiness with her living arrangement. When children are school age, they frequently protest a move away from their old school and neighborhood. This tension often calls for hard decisions about the anticipated move. Can a parent defer moving into a more desirable home or is the move a crucial one?

Q.: Have you ever had to define your own needs in terms of your child?

Martha:

When I was still married and wanted a separation, I worried about Toni being fatherless. When I needed to go to work, I felt guilty about leaving him in child care. But I knew if I was unhappy, I would be less of a mother. My mother constantly talked about self-sacrifice, always shorted herself, and all she accomplished was creating guilt.

I decided to leave my husband. I felt much better and more comfortable. I wasn't being criticized, so there was more consistency in Toni's handling. I was happier. I could give my son more attention.

This mother's worries about choosing between her need to leave a marriage and, out of necessity, return to work, and her son's relationship with his father delayed her decision for more than a year. This waiting period may be valuable as a time for clarifying needs. By the time she had made the decision to leave the marriage, she felt firm in her decision and more prepared to handle her son's reaction and needs. She had wanted to move some distance away to start her new life but made the compromise of remaining in the same area as her husband so that her ex-husband and son could spend weekends together.

Heather:

Sometimes it's a trade-off of needs. Sometimes I need less or more than my children, and I am trying not to feel so desperate about grabbing time they may really need. For instance, I have arranged for a whole day off from both of them every Wednesday. I have guarded that day with a zeal—the thought of my kids getting sick on that day has terrorized me . . . but this Wednesday, I found I was able to let my oldest child stay with me because he had a bad week and didn't want to go to child care. We shopped and ate lunch and went to a movie. I wanted to go home and do my own work. I wanted to have my hair cut. But it seemed OK not to do those things this one time and wait until next week.

It is often so hard to decide that we need time away from our family that we cling to this time rigidly as if it would vanish completely should we ever miss it. We can just as easily lock ourselves into patterns of mechanically meeting needs as mechanically denying them.

Paying attention to the warning signs

If we don't pay attention to the warning signs within ourselves that our needs are being ignored, we may find ourselves in situations where we lose control. All is not lost should we explode. We can use an emotional crisis as an opportunity to reappraise needs, especially the denied ones.

The following narrative was written by the woman whose effort to understand her volatile shadow parent and to develop a more realistic ideal for herself as a parent was first described in the chapter on personal myths.

Carla:

One day several months after the birth of my second child, my four-year-old daughter was being unusually irrational. She was refusing to take her nap and I was very much in need of a nap myself. I had worked all morning as a parent assistant at her nursery school class. She was screaming at me, refusing to lie down, and kicking me if I tried to carry her. After several moments of total frustration I shouted, "If you don't go take your nap I'm going to leave and never come back!"

Several hours later my stomach twisted up in knots of guilt, for I felt I had said one of the worst things you can say to a child. I was certain I had planted the seed of lifelong insecurity in her. I called a hot line for parents in our city. I apologized profusely for calling with such an insignificant problem and attempted to sound as though I was a competent mother—though I felt helpless, totally inadequate. After all, I am a well-educated, middle-class *teacher*. I should be able to handle the demands and irrationalities of a four-year-old.

I was referred to a mothers' discussion/therapy group, which I still attend (one year and another child later). It hasn't changed my child-rearing techniques dramatically, but it has given me the encouragement I needed to find part-time child care for my kids. Now I have one day a week away from them. At first, when I took them to the sitter I had a gnawing ache in my stomach all day, and I would use the time away from them to go shopping (for them) or do housework. I realize I was trying to justify the separation from them. Though I still get a twinge of guilt when I kiss them good-bye, I have given up the housework and present buying for a real "day off." I only do things and go places for myself.

I look forward to that day, especially when all three kids are demanding my attention and I am attempting to make dinner and do the day's accumulation of dishes. I say to myself, "Ah, only two, three, four, et cetera, more days until I can take off and become the young, attractive, outgoing, gregarious woman I remember being five years ago." It has lessened the tension and feeling of drowning in other people's needs that drove me to scream and lash out uncontrollably at my kids.

Closing words

Helen:

I like to hold my children and feel close to them that way. I worry that I won't get that close feeling I need when they stop wanting me to be physical with them. Will I feel the same way just sitting with my hands in my lap and talking to them?

Dee:

Sometimes everything I do with and for my children makes me feel good about them and about myself. Some days everything I do for them is out of a sense of duty.

6. Learning from Crisis

We do not welcome crisis into our lives. But the process of recognizing the warning signs of crisis and finding the help we need offers us the healing gift of growth.

Because crisis is an uninvited guest, we cannot necessarily breathe easily because we escaped the "baby blues" or weathered the first adolescence of a two-year-old. The dangerous denial of needs, the accumulation of stress, the sudden tragedy can happen to the parent of an eight-year-old or to the parent of a young adult as well. No matter when such crises occur, there are common patterns of discovery and recovery. "What crisis may mean is simply that the old style of living is no longer adequate to deal with the increased stress . . . this opens the possibility of developing new and better ways of dealing with stress. . . . Crisis is a dangerous opportunity for positive growth."[1]

Parenting is a role fraught with stress. When we confront additional stress—increased, unexpected, or devastating pressure and pain—we also can find ourselves in the midst of an emotional crisis. How does daily stress evolve into crisis? When crisis strikes—gradually or suddenly—how do we respond? What are some of the ways we can work through personal crisis with renewed strength and insights into ourselves?

If we follow Jacob's mother, interviewed in Chapter 2,

through her postpartum crisis, we will be able to see some patterns. In that interview we shared in some detail the experience of a young mother whose postpartum period was a personal disaster. Her expectations for herself as a parent and the picture she had formed of her daily life with an infant were radically dissimilar from the reality of her relationship with that baby. Within a few weeks after the birth of her child she found herself heading for a full-blown crisis: reeling, confused, depressed, and at times not able to cope with the drastic changes.

What precipitates crisis?

The postpartum period is frequently experienced as a crisis by mothers, partly because of the vacillating of female hormonal levels immediately after birth, but also largely because of the stresses bearing down on them at this point.

James Coleman, in his *Abnormal Psychology and Modern Life,* has isolated five common sources of severe stress.[2] All five existed for that particular postpartum mother during her first few months of parenthood. She was flooded with the following feelings:

1. *Failure,* in an endeavor in which she was emotionally involved—raising her child. This type of personal failure, with high stakes for success, Coleman sees as being particularly devaluating and stressful.

From those first hours home from the hospital, as she fumbled with diaper pins and a squalling, miserable infant who could not be placated, she saw herself as having totally failed in her mothering role. Surrounded by media pictures of smoothly confident motherhood, with the promise that with the proper plastic diaper and baby lotion all would be well, she felt keenly aware of her:

2. *Personal limitations and lack of resources.* Rocking her baby, passing the hours watching daytime television,

she witnessed a parade of media mothers and soap opera stars handling their motherhood with smiling ease. Their houses were as immaculate and well organized as hers had been before the baby came home. She felt herself smothering in a mountain of diapers, drowning in juice bottles, crusted dishes, and soiled clothing. What was their secret? What was their advantage? They must have household help! Why couldn't she be like those other mothers?

3. *Loss.* In this case she did not suffer a material or personal loss, as through death of spouse, divorce, or marital separation (the three most stressful events reported by adults in this society). But she did experience a loss of social status, in her own mind, when she quit graduate school and turned her energies toward full-time parenting. Especially, she sustained loss because she traded a sense of accomplishment and relatively high status in the academic world for uncertainty and real status diminishment. In her college community, parenting was a role of little consequence.

When she found that she did not feel the pleasure in being with her baby and caring for him that she had anticipated and that she felt society expected of her, when there were moments she felt great rage at that tiny red-faced dictator and at her husband for his absence and his inability to diminish her misery, she also experienced:

4. *Guilt.* She was convinced that her angry and resentful feelings for her baby and husband were "wrong" in the most basic moral sense, and she felt helpless to will those feelings away. Prolonged guilt, without any ritualistic methods of exorcising it, can be one of the most profound causes of self-recrimination and anxiety and can lead to a severe crisis.

She had traded a life-style of crowded city bus rides and a bustling campus for a third-floor walk-up apartment and its murmuring silences. She knew no other mothers, she saw none walking down the streets, and, at first, she was not motivated to search for peers or other social outlets.

In the first couple of months of her baby's life, she often felt engulfed in:

5. *Loneliness.* Just as her baby had need for a daily diet of love and caring, she needed renewed human contact and nurturing. Her husband was not able to provide the time and support necessary to soothe and heal her. He did not fully understand this new experience or the depth of her crisis.

Failure, personal limitations, loss, guilt, and loneliness —all these severe stresses were at work during that post-partum period. How profoundly this mother was affected by this multiple stress had to do with her own personal resources. Her response was colored by her individual tolerance of stress and frustration, which, like pain tolerance during labor, varies greatly. And, importantly, her reaction depended on the viability of her coping mechanisms, or the ways in which she protected herself from slipping into the disequilibrium of crisis.

The stages of crisis

The Cocoanut Grove fire in Boston in 1942 provided Eric Lindemann with an opportunity to study the grief responses of people who had lost loved ones and to produce a theoretic framework, also developed by Gerald Caplan, now known as crisis theory.[3] This theory breaks down the components of crisis and puts together an approach to helping people through a crisis. As in all facets of parenting—raising ourselves as well as our children—knowledge of the mechanics of crisis can help us to be aware of the development of our own crises.

Crisis theory examines coping mechanisms that offer us some protection against everyday stresses. We all develop idiosyncratic coping styles that work for us. For example, the postpartum mother might have employed repression, kept herself unaware, held in check her feelings of disappointment, failure, anger, and resentment for as long as this mechanism worked to control the pressures in her life. She might have reacted by rationalization, convinced herself that there were valid reasons having nothing to do with her—lack of money or proper housing or equipment —for her feelings of failure and her inability to keep on top of her situation. Or, through projection, she might have laid the blame on her husband for not providing enough support, or on society for tricking her into a false picture of motherhood, or on her baby for being an impossibly difficult child.

There are endless variations on these typical coping styles, including apathy, a denial of the importance and effect of the stress—and learning, a growth out of the stress into a new style of dealing with life.

How healthy these coping styles are in the long run for our total emotional growth is not as important as their usefulness in helping us to maintain control in the face of the stress we sometimes experience. When coping gives way to crisis, those coping mechanisms that have worked for us in the past are no longer a match for the stresses we now face. It is at this point that we enter a state of crisis.

According to crisis theory, the first stage of crisis starts with stress, which threatens that precarious balance we have worked to create within ourselves. If our normal responses work for us, then we have averted further crisis.

If our tried-and-true resources fail, the crisis escalates and we begin to work on the problem in an effort to deal with the stress. We may find that by focusing on the key stress we can come up with a solution in fairly short order. This postpartum mother, when she found her ordinary responses ineffective, could come up with no new coping patterns to deal with this unfamiliar and unanticipated stress. She could not see clearly through the maze of stresses, most of them new to her, to focus on and sort them out.

If concentration on the problem works, or if the most troublesome stress evaporates (for instance, if her poorly sleeping and irritable baby had suddenly begun napping on schedule and crying less, giving her some breathing space), then the crisis is stopped at this point in its development. If we find we lack the internal resources to deal with the stress, the crisis continues and we may turn to external resources—family or friends or professional counsel. If we are given and accept appropriate help at this point, the crisis can be resolved.

If for some reason there are no external resources, or if they are ineffective, then the fourth stage of crisis develops. The symptoms can be suicide, severe depression, psychotic disturbance, running away, flight into drugs and alcohol.

How do we experience crisis?

Postpartum disturbances range from the highly common blue period to severe depression and psychotic states. However, in some cases, such mild reactions might progress almost imperceptibly to deep depression. A mother may express a lack of interest in her infant, have fears it will be harmed, or show great underlying hostility toward her husband.[4]

Joan told us, "When Mathew was about ten days old, I suddenly started worrying about a fire in our house, that the baby would be burned. I had to go buy a fire extinguisher. I worried about that a lot."

Meg said, "After Emily was born, I sank into a depression. I worried all the time about money . . . about my baby when I had to leave her to go to work . . . about what I was doing with my life . . . about my marriage. . . . Meeting some friends literally kept me from suicide."

And a family crisis counselor told us, "First-time mothers seem to go through the depression and ignore it. It surfaces after two or three years when the stress of submerging needs accumulates to a breaking or explosion point. This is the point at which I see abuse and other unsuccessful responses and coping mechanisms."

Mary B. is a counselor with Parental Stress, a group that works with parents in crisis who frequently but not always cry for help by physically abusing their children. In her position as a group leader of peer support groups—parents who share the experience of potential or,actual child abuse—she has come to see some common points of crisis:

- lover/husband relationship problems
- financial crisis/welfare problems
- the birth of a second or third child
- unwanted pregnancies
- illness of a family member
- death of a family member
- identity

As discussed in the chapter on identity, this last crisis may occur when parental roles need to change. "This change in how a parent views her role can be caused by personal pain, media influences, or the modeling of other women."

Many of these crises are universally felt, regardless of whether a person is a parent or not: death, serious illness in a loved one, alienation and separation from a loved one are stresses of greatest magnitude. But crisis can also arise from something so small that our pride won't let us acknowledge it as a crisis.

Disappointments, like failing to get a raise or to do well on an examination, seem little reason to slip into crisis when compared to the serious situations just described, but when added to the daily demands and the heavy responsibility of child raising, these events can be shattering.

Money difficulties are also compounded when children's welfare is at stake, and when freedom to move, take new jobs, juggle life-styles is doubly, even triply, complicated. For single parents, often the stress of separation and divorce is promptly increased by new financial burdens. Frustration, loss, guilt, loneliness, envy of others' status all come into play—and are precursors of deep crisis.

Overwhelmed, confused, and uncertain how best to utilize our personal resources or how and where to seek support—this kind of devastating multiple stress can cause us to latch onto harmful and ultimately unsuccessful new coping mechanisms.

Unsuccessful coping

Among the unsuccessful coping styles are misdirected anger—in the forms of physical and/or verbal abuse toward children, spouse, and other adults in a family; barbiturate usage—"the Valium syndrome"; and alcoholism. Some parents handle crisis by developing an "I don't care" attitude toward their children and family responsibilities; they become defiant, resist help, and then suffer an accompanying guilt about their performance as parents. This often causes a chain reaction of violent anger which in turn leads to more guilt.

Other parents in crisis respond with "the hell with it." They drop out, either actually leaving a family situation or mentally fantasizing about a permanent retreat.

Parents can also ignore the source of pain, numb themselves to their distress, continue their daily routines, until they lose contact with what causes their unhappiness.

Through the maze: unraveling and growth

At this point in our story the picture appears dismal, the prognosis is uncertain and discouraging for an individual or family in crisis. Far from it. At this crucial stage positive growth can begin. "The dangerous opportunity" in crisis is that potential for either prolonged destructive functioning or a blossoming of new and better ways to approach life.

The course of crisis for an individual depends first on that person's own ego strength, a factor that counseling and peer support has no control over, and second, on the influences available at her time of crisis. Crisis theory maintains that persons in crisis are extremely vulnerable to external influences and most open to constructive advice.

Our original postpartum mother, overwhelmed by stress, isolated and lost, was given just that kind of support by a public health group for mothers of young children. There she found peer counsel, companionship, and leadership by a skilled public health nurse. She was ripe for getting hold of the scattered pieces of herself and her life, for taking a closer look at the dynamics of her family; where her husband needed to take a more active and supportive role, where she needed to lower expectations and relax her goals, and where she might restructure her days to allow some respite from an exhausting stage in her child's development.

A peer support group, such as the one she discovered through a newspaper article, offers one vehicle for the direct expression of feelings and positive direction. These groups are not, in most instances, intensive therapy groups under the direction of psychologists or psychiatrists; they are led by people whose training is in offering short-term counseling. What parents in crisis get from this source is a release in talking, an awareness of community among group members, and the experience of being heard and understood.

As we have discussed before, many parents feel that "good parents" do not show their emotions around their children. Through group discussion, example, and support, parents in crisis learn to share their pain or grief or anger with their families. They learn to tell themselves and their children that all those intense feelings are OK. Convincing a parent that showing emotion is a human and acceptable response to events can break the pattern of repression that leads to great explosions. Children who grow up in a home where feelings are always private are likely to fall into the same destructive pattern.

Other forms of crisis intervention

Crisis intervention has emerged as a response to a widespread and increasing need for immediate help for individuals and families who find themselves in highly stressful situations. Traditional therapy may be too slow a route, with its delays in scheduling that first appointment and treatment over a sustained period of time; it may not meet the needs of individuals in crisis. When people find themselves unable to deal with stress by themselves and have exhausted or have found useless the counsel of family and friends, they are now able in many communities to turn to "Band-Aid" crisis therapy, which offers face-to-face discussion or twenty-four-hour telephone hot lines, manned by a combination of professionals and trained volunteers. One woman told us about her experience:

One afternoon, when my husband was away on one of his frequent long business trips, my six-year-old had been making demands on me since lunchtime. I had been working increased hours that month because of some financial setbacks, was tired, depressed, overwrought. I had sent him to his room so many times for sassing me and making those demands. . . . I thought I was going to kill him if I touched him. It really scared me. I remembered about the parent hot line in our town. I closed the door to my room, dialed, and let it all out. I found myself sobbing, pouring out more than that volunteer probably could understand, pulling myself together, making sense to myself, getting away from my kids . . . crying for the first time in years.

In this situation, the parent found satisfaction in relating her problems and feelings and in working through some temporary solutions for herself in a remarkably short period of time. For others, the crisis counselor therapist must play a more active role. Crisis seems to demand active response: help in clarifying the problem, suggestions for plans of action, reassurances, and concrete information and support for parents in crisis. Passive "mirroring" of feelings and problems is often not enough at this time. A hot line counselor in Berkeley, California, said, "They want some options clearly stated. They're unable to come up, at this point, with their own."

During this short-term counseling, a parent should not expect a comprehensive, long-range personality evaluation or a drastic change in coping styles. The goal is rather to find some effective method of handling crisis, to get through the trauma in one piece. A side effect sometimes is that we produce within ourselves brilliant, effective new ways of reacting to stress, and phenomenal growth.

It should be emphasized that crisis can also produce positive change on the strength of our own ability to delve into our hidden resources. It does not necessarily go the route we have mapped—with an inevitable need for therapeutic support—informal or institutional. One mother describes the journey through crisis she made alone:

When we moved five hundred miles away from all family and friends, taking our children from their loved home and neighborhood, their peers and schools, I was terrified. I started acting in ways, clinging to securities, some of them destructive, that I hadn't in years. But I would deny that my behavior was about moving. I felt helpless, there was nothing I could do about it. I felt I always needed outside support, and that leaving those people was a threat to my whole being. I felt anguished.

It wasn't until some time after the move that I realized the crisis was exhilarating—I did fine without my friends. I surprised myself with my self-sufficiency, endurance, lack of dependency really. It was important for me to acknowledge those things, because I started to see myself in a new way. If we hadn't moved, I never would have known those insecurities didn't exist anymore. They were like ghosts, and seeing them made them disappear. Seeing my own crisis this way also helped me make it a growth experience for my children. I could reinforce all their developing resourcefulness and adaptability to change.

We all struggle our own way through crisis, some finding the support of peers, family, or counseling sufficient. Others may need long-term therapy to reach our ultimate goals. If our postpartum mother in crisis had as her central problem a lack of self-esteem, the relief of pain would have been a stopgap. Once having passed through the acute pain, she would benefit from a long-term examination and treatment of the problem.

Crisis counselors and an increasing number of therapists place strong emphasis on using the support of other family members. Virginia Satir, in *Conjoint Family Therapy*, discusses the fluid balance within a family that makes it function smoothly. When crisis erupts, from external or internal causes, one person or another may be particularly victimized by this imbalance.

While Ms. Satir concentrates in this text on children as the family members in crisis, what she says can be true of the adults as well: ". . . his symptoms are a message he is distorting his own growth as a result of trying to alleviate and absorb his parent's pain."[5]

Through self-awareness and outside clinical help, an individual can develop some methods of dealing with pain, only to be tossed back into an unhealthy family setting. When the entire family, including children old enough to verbalize, involve themselves in crisis therapy or in long-term family therapy, that precious, precarious family balance and overall health can be restored.

How family members can help one another to handle stress creatively

Caplan, in his study of families with premature infants,[6] characterized families who handle crisis constructively as ones that:

1. allow and encourage the family member to deal with the crisis rather than ignore it, in the sense of urging him to gather information and resources as well as express feelings;

2. permit the person time out from role responsibilities, with other people filling in effectively, but also call the person back into the stream of things after a suitable interim, not allow him to "float";

3. avoid blaming people inside or outside the family for the crisis;

4. have good communication about "who will do what" in terms of role responsibility during crisis;

5. do not deny the crisis and pretend to ignore it; they see themselves as able to affect it.

The dangerous opportunity that crisis provides can be a stepping-stone to better individual and family balance and health. We need to be aware of the kinds of pressures parenting (and modern living in general) brings, the unexpected stresses that, layered with the challenges of our daily lives, can send us down the road toward severe crisis, and the options available for dealing with crisis when it strikes. "Often it takes a real crisis to bring out a sure knowledge of the real inner self, and it is always a creative knowledge."[7]

Interviews

Postpartum

The following story is another mother's experience of severe postpartum depression and her steps out of this crisis.

Meg, age 34; child, age 6:

I had no intention of going back, but I guess I must have sensed the necessity because I had taken a maternity leave instead of quitting. I was so depressed and we were so broke . . . I worried all the time about money. I had to go back. I hired someone to care for Emily. I paid more than the going rate then for somebody who would do right by my sweet baby. . . . I got up at five A.M. to get her ready. I wanted to keep nursing her as long as I could so I would nurse her before we left. We didn't have a car then, so I had to take one bus to drop her at the sitter's and walk with her and all her things two blocks to the sitter's apartment. I was in a sweat by the time I even got on the bus to go to the city. It took me three buses to get to work, and then I would have to turn around again. I sat down and figured out that I ended up with about a dollar fifty an hour after child care and bus fare. I quit after eight weeks and came home. I was so glad to be back home with my baby that I wasn't so depressed, except that while I was working my milk dried up and I couldn't nurse anymore. I had really wanted to keep nursing.

After a while I reached a plateau. I found a friend, an ally, and we would take walks together with our

babies and talk. We had common feelings and experiences in our personal lives at that time also. It
literally, I believe, kept me from suicide. Another
friend got together a play group when Emily was
eight months old, and out of this group we formed a
women's group. We all were interested in writing a
book on the first year of mothering—how ripped off,
scared, and frustrated we often felt, all the adjust-
ments in your marriage, sexually and otherwise. That
never took off, but the group helped for a while.

Getting myself out of that deep depression was a
slow process. If you are depressed, you don't have
the energy to pull yourself out and follow the steps.
But later I realized the steps involved:

1. Getting out of the house.

2. Being around other people.

3. Widening your interests. It was hard for me to
be out there in the world looking for work, so I found
ways to stay home and support myself. Now I'm feeling a little braver, and am going to venture out a little
more.

4. Developing my own feminist consciousness. I
started to examine and rebel against some of the
stereotypes in myself. I began to view myself with
more respect. I saw that I was good with babies and
not everyone is.

Jane, age 38; two sons, ages 14, 12:

My first experience as a mother was problematic
from the beginning. My first son was physically uncomfortable all the time; he cried all the time. I had
a mechanical idea that someone could always fix what
was wrong. During the first year I couldn't seem to fix
anything. Other people must have felt the same way,
because they were always trying to pinpoint what
was wrong with him. People would tell me, "He must

be wet," or, "He must be hungry." And when I could not meet his needs, when he wouldn't stop crying, I responded to the blame.

He had pneumonia several times as a small baby, and when he was a year and a half, the doctors discovered he had blocked tubes in his ears—which caused him to have splitting headaches. I was upset that he hadn't been tested sooner—that we hadn't both been spared a lot of pain.

When I found out I was pregnant again, I could not see how I could manage. I went through some therapy at that time to try to get myself together enough to cope with the prospect of handling two children. But right from the beginning, Kent was much less difficult, like he was the way he was supposed to be.

Before Kent was born, Brian had two operations and he was a lot better. He was still prone to tonsil troubles and had allergies to many foods. I went back to work because I had come completely apart trying to manage all this, and he stayed with his grandmother while I was away. Going back to work at that time was a saving thing.

Some babies are troubled with extraordinary physical discomforts during their first year. It is especially difficult for us to know what to do for our babies when they cannot verbalize their pain.

Allergic children present both doctors and parents with a labyrinth of symptoms, and untangling these takes what seems to us, as parents of unhappy babies, a good deal of time.

We will often feel frustrated and incompetent and physically drained. It is important to be aware that we are by no means alone.

Barbara:

The second child was always more difficult. She's been a poor sleeper. I didn't have the concentrated time to spend with her. There was more drudgery, more housework, more competition for my attention. Kim was more tractable, Tamar more stubborn. In the past six months things have changed, the marriage has improved, I'm feeling much happier. I've made my peace with my second child. I'm spending more time with her alone. I found that during that period when I really needed to get away, the more I tried being away, the crabbier she would be, and it was a vicious circle. When I was around, she was much happier.

A crisis can be brought about by unexpected changes in your life.

June:

I worked and was away from her so much, the time I had with her was precious to me. At eighteen months she got defiant. She was willful. It was difficult for me to decide how to handle it. You don't want to squash all that is spontaneous in your child. One never resolves it. It's a matter of compromise. I know many parents are more forceful, but I try to give her some choices, so we can solve problems together.

Sometimes our decisions have unexpected consequences.

Meredith:

We did have a very large problem with her sleeping when she was around two. My mother was ill, and I had to go be with her twice for four days. The second time I came back she cried all night, screamed.

This continued for three months. It took her one and a half months to sleep at all at night. I was so fatigued I was beginning to fall apart, and I was concerned about what I had done to cause my child to be this way. Although I felt I had been careful and conscientious in preparing to leave her and leaving her with people she knew, I still felt I had somehow failed.

I finally went to the doctor, who gave her some sleeping medication. I only tried it a few days, but it didn't seem to work. And I didn't feel good about solving the problem that way. Then I began to give her little presents if she slept. After three weeks, I just put a star on a chart for every night she slept. She still tended to wake up at night, but much less often. Eventually, somewhere around two and a half, she stopped waking.

For a year and a half I didn't leave her again. We didn't even go out at night for a long time. It might not have upset her, but it seemed right to us not to distress her again.

Understanding a child's developmental characteristics and needs can help us rearrange priorities in our lives.

Elizabeth:

Tom had begun to do some stealing. When visitors would come, they began to tell us that money was missing from their wallets and purses. He would give some of it to his younger brother to keep him quiet. When confronted about it, he would deny everything.

When we came back we found a nice house, a good school with good teachers—but we hadn't really examined the student body. The first few months went well; when we came back, we had all talked about self-discipline and inner strength, and Tom seemed to be listening. We didn't threaten him—we tried to trust him.

He came to us and asked if he could take a job as a baby-sitter, which meant his leaving school early every day. We said yes, and later regretted having devalued school for the value of earning money. He started hanging around with a peer group where he baby-sat, all into a variety of petty crimes and dope. We found packages in his closet that he had evidently shoplifted. He would deny it. Last Christmas we drove around and talked about how he was messing up what he—and we—could have here. My ex-husband did not support him being in this community—he feels it is too "loose" here—and Tom was living a life that supported this feeling.

The final straw for us came when he was caught late at night with burglary tools climbing the fire escape outside a local bank. He and his friend said they were just messing around. The police did not charge him with as serious a crime as they might, but I thought about what I needed to do. I could not believe anything he told me anymore. I had no effect with him. I wrote his father and Tom went with him. I felt really disappointed. I had tried hard with my son, and it wasn't worth it. I didn't feel any sense of personal loss or regret—just a tremendous sense of relief, like a hurricane was out of the house.

He calls now and seems to be doing OK—he's working out a system of values for himself now. His new environment is very conservative, fundamentally religious, old-fashioned in family ways.

There had been no family counseling available to Tom and his parents in their early years of difficulties. By the time he was in serious trouble, the *dynamic* between him and his mother and stepfather was poor and communication had deteriorated. Usually it is the troubled *dynamic* between particular family members that can cause a breakdown of communication and crisis.

Removing Tom from this situation into a different—in his case a more authoritarian—setting helped enormously.

Crisis after divorce

Sue:

The first time I went to a crisis group I thought I had no problem, compared with everyone else. I was just another divorced person. Then I realized that whatever was going on inside me was a real crisis—it didn't have to be compared with anyone else. One of the nicest things about being in a group—you have feelings—other people respond to them—it helped because they had the same feelings. You can feel very alone in a crisis.

Alice, age 35; two daughters, ages 10, 6:

I guess I would define crisis as involving a big change profoundly affecting us in everyday life. These adjectives describe my divorce. It involves a decision about change, it involves making a decision that constitutes all the stress.

Divorce meant the death of a relationship, the end of a unit, the four of us. I felt I had the responsibility for reconciling each individual involved to the fact we wouldn't be living together anymore. I just took it upon myself as the "mother" of the group. After we made our decision, we stayed in the house another month. We had to deal with the sadness of ending the relationship. Above all, I wanted to see the girls come through with as little hurt as possible. The worst thing I could feel was guilt. I wanted to look back and feel I did my very best for them. I tried to cut off empathy for my husband.

I could define some stages I went through during this time. The first stage involved a year of knowing I should be terminating the relationship, but lacking the self-confidence to do it—loss of self-esteem, self-respect, because I allowed myself to be treated in a way I shouldn't.

Stage two: getting the nerve to leave—and doing it. I felt better about myself once I made my decision, I never wavered. I cut emotional ties with him —I was glad I had left him. It helped me in my feelings about myself.

I lived alone for several months. My decision was made. My husband would drop by for hours at night to talk. His goal was to get us back together.

Finally, I allowed myself to consider going back for everyone's sake (except mine). I went to a marriage counselor alone. I saw her just once. She said not to go back unless he agreed to see a counselor also. He began to threaten me.

I didn't want to call my parents. They had never been through anything like that. My only refuge was the man I had been seeing.

My parents' good opinion was all that was holding me together, I stayed with them for about ten days.

Our friends were all mutual friends. They all had children and lives of their own. I never had a confidante. I never turned to anyone.

Stage three: I didn't let him see the kids for three months after he had threatened me. I finally called him and faced him. We made an agreement that he wouldn't come near me. I had to deal with fear at this point. I was alone. I was a full-time parent. We had always shared in all responsibilities. It was a good period. Things were no longer up in the air. I had the kids, and he accepted that.

Stage four: he called and told me the fight was over. He would stop seeing the lawyer, stop trying to get the kids. Finally, on Easter, I let them see him. I was terrified he wouldn't bring them back, but he did. At first he saw them every Sunday, then after a year he started taking them every weekend. It happened naturally; he wanted it and they wanted it. It's not like I'm a mother and he's a father—we're both parents. That's the way it is when you're separate.

When I was married I was a mother and a wife. I had almost totally lost my own identity except for these two roles. A whole new person emerged through this crisis—*me*. I hadn't tried to do anything except better myself as a wife and mother. That other person was locked away with no channels to emerge. I kept flashing back to eighteen and seventeen, a long time back, to figure why that was when I was last a person. At first I was so overwhelmed by the crisis I couldn't see the benefits of it aside from being out of a bad marital situation. Then I needed to work it out, ask why everything had happened. I locked it away until I could deal with it. I devoted energy to my rebirth. I felt I had a clean slate. It was exciting deciding what I could do with myself. I had such great hope. I felt so free.

Alice's story is one of a woman going through one of the most severe adult crises, almost literally without the counsel and support of anyone. Yet she had the strength to work her way out of a difficult period, with a sense of clarity, purpose, and hope.

Entering the world of the disabled child

This family entered the world of the disabled and found through crisis the strength and sensitivity to locate the help they needed. They discovered their own ability to make decisions about her care and education. They discovered the support system they already had in their nuclear and extended family. They plunged into a world of trauma and fear and came out whole.

Jackie Brand; two daughters, ages 7, 3:

I have a daughter, Shoshana, who was born three and a half years ago with a heart defect. When she was eight months old, she required heart surgery, during which she sustained brain damage. That damage left her with paralysis and cortical blindness. We still don't know the extent of the damage. Immediately after surgery, our concerns centered on survival. Once it had become clear to us that she would survive and she began the long process of recuperation, we began searching for programs and for feedback about others' experience, in order to help us define what Shoshana needed, and how to begin working toward her rehabilitation and development.

During the days of crisis at the hospital, I was totally thrown out of my small world. My life before Shoshana's birth left me totally oblivious to all but the nondisabled. Though I would have had a polite response to anyone's questions about the rights of the disabled, in fact, I had been unaware of and unconcerned with those basic needs which now totally absorb me. From a world which concerned itself with normalcy, with intact, healthy children, I moved into one which revolved around crisis, trauma, and disability. Now the outside "normal" world seemed alien to me. During that period I didn't want to see anyone who hadn't experienced some of what I was experiencing and what Shoshana was experiencing. I felt I could only communicate with those that were living with similar fears and anxieties. It was very painful saying good-bye to the presurgery Shoshana —crawling, standing, seeing. I had to greet another child who could neither see nor move. It seemed that only those people who were experiencing those days with me could possibly understand the depth of my emotion. And I didn't want to share my feelings. It was very difficult to reach out to my friends. I wanted their support and understanding, but I feared their pity.

After the first couple of months of recuperation, we began searching for infant programs. Shoshana was ten months old, and the neurologist suggested that she might benefit from an infant stimulation program. In retrospect, I realize that infant programs are largely parent support groups. Shoshana didn't seem to respond to the program, nor did the program offer what she needed. We didn't know what she needed either. But for a while, the support and understanding we got, particularly from other parents in similar situations, was helpful. The group sessions helped me begin to sort out the new balance in my life.

One of these new realities was the effect, both positive and negative, of Shoshana's disabilities on her older sister, Michelle. It's hard to estimate how Michelle has been affected. At seven years of age she has been exposed to emotions, expectations, and information that even an adult would have (and did have) trouble absorbing. I don't believe that she will ever grow up wearing the same blinders about disability that I wore. While I neither can nor want to exclude Michelle from the concerns we share as a family, I must constantly look at how I've balanced those concerns with Michelle's needs. I am Michelle's mother as much as I am Shoshana's mother.

Because our family unit, both nuclear and extended, is so strong, our needs for external support soon decreased, and we began to feel an urgency about programs for Shoshana. She had begun to regain some vision, and we were anxious to build on what strength and abilities were there. Steve and I spent the following year in energetic pursuit of programs that might help her. We investigated everything, trying not to reject or resist anything. We enrolled in training courses, attended conferences and workshops, went to innumerable meetings, and spoke with a multitude of professionals.

After a year of looking for the "experts," I began to realize that in fact we had the clearest notion about Shoshana and her needs. All the professionals —neurologists, cardiologists, ophthalmologists, child development specialists, et cetera, looked at a piece of our daughter. Their views depended on their specialties; no one looked at the total child. I had to trust my own feelings about her in order to get beyond the fragmented perspective of the professional world. Any program she might attend would only consume a small part of her day, whereas we were with her most of the time. We had to be clear about what we were doing and try to make decisions about what would work and what wouldn't. It takes time to build the confidence in yourself which is necessary in order to make decisions. Taking the decisions away from the professionals and putting them in your own hands is both frightening and isolating. But you begin to rely on your own strengths and to trust your own perceptions.

Shoshana is a loving and delightful child. She faces

special challenges, as does our whole family. She responds to these challenges well, and these experiences make her a special person. My role as parent, though sometimes difficult and often unique, is certainly exciting and full.

"A moment-by-moment thing"

What meaning can we derive from a spouse's death? A sense of strong shared values concerning the meaning of life can be the wellspring from which we draw our strength.

Elinor, age 33, widow; son, age 9:

Charles was going to an outpatient clinic for tests. The night before he was scheduled for a liver scan he was kept awake by the first attack of acute and unmistakable pain. I stayed home from work. It was Easter vacation and David was home from school.

The seriousness of what was going on must have been immediately apparent to the medical staff. I overheard him whisperingly referred to as the young man with the enormous liver.

David started to cry when we had to leave the hospital without Charles. We'd been there for hours that morning and into the afternoon. He said, "I don't want Dad to die!" I explained that he just had to stay for more tests.

Although the doctor had known before, he waited until Monday morning to give us the diagnosis. Carcinoma of the colon with metastasis to three-quarters of the liver. I was privately told the prognosis. Six months.

My whole sense of time and space seemed to drop into an abyss. The world felt enormous and without structure or dimension.

Charles was appalled at the thought of telling David. He thought if we even said the word *cancer,* people would relay horror stories and frighten him.

Charles remained in the hospital for two more weeks of chemotherapy. He found hospital life distasteful and an infringement of his freedom and dignity. He decided he was never going to be hospitalized again. He wasn't.

During those two weeks David seemed to adjust well and appeared calm. He made special get-well cards for Charles. Since children weren't allowed to visit patients on the third floor, I would bring one of David's friends along and the boys would busy themselves watching television and running around the lobby.

When Charles came home from the hospital, he was quite weak. He was a big man and it was unusual to see him like that. He was optimistic and appeared to be regaining his strength during the first month. He went to the outpatient clinic twice a week for a blood test and chemotherapy shot. By the second and third months his symptoms were getting worse. Most of the doctors avoided him and he became more and more agitated, nervous, and angry. Charles went through many of the stages described in the death and dying field today—shock, withdrawal, anger, fear, and acceptance.

Charles had been diagnosed at the beginning of April. By July his health was obviously deteriorating. Chemotherapy wasn't helping. As a last resort, we went to a clinic in Mexico. Perhaps it was a reflection of our state of mind, but it was one of the most desolate places I have ever been. Charles was forced to acknowledge fully his upcoming passing and I, with him, was forced to face and acknowledge that I knew. It was a very painful and sad time.

Despite our sadness, David seemed happy on the surface. I remember him popping up in the window of our first-floor hotel apartment, trying to surprise us with a big smile on his face, an enormous sombrero on his head—seemingly oblivious to the tears in the room. He busied himself playing with the Mexican children he met.

There was no reason to remain in Mexico. Charles's main concern became hourly and daily. If he was to die, he wanted to go in the comforts of his own home and among the friends he knew and loved. He was anxious to return quickly. As we drove back, Charles was incredibly agitated and in pain but became calm and comfortable and happier the closer we got to Pasadena. He was beaming when we finally pulled into our town. We'd made it! He insisted we stop to visit some of his special friends before going home. David was sleeping.

Our return from Mexico marked the final stage and the beginning of our farewell. Charles changed physically every day, his big frame becoming more and more skeletal, supporting an abdomen large enough to contain a nine-month fetus. Our house was open and friends came often. Our life was lived in the living room where Charles ate, kept company, slept, and received his shots. Death and dying was an open topic of discussion and an event that Charles not only discussed but anticipated with growing relief. As time passed and good-byes were said, his life turned more to a world we couldn't see and his departure seemed imminent. He became incredibly sweet and extremely sensitive to the slightest suggestion of disharmony or disagreement. He delighted in children. (I remember one little girl who was a bit overwhelmed by the bear hug he gave her.)

David and I talked. He started to cry when I said,

"Dad is very sick." He said he knew. We had a strong conviction that there is a purpose to life and that death is simply the other side of the same coin. It helped to already have a language for our experience and it enabled us to talk openly about it as a change of one suit of clothes for another. I can't imagine being able to cope without a conviction that could sustain and give meaning to what otherwise would have been an overwhelmingly sad experience. It enabled us to feel we were indeed part of a greater whole, a master plan. Charles's very being seemed to radiate this and it was as though we were all allowed to share in a very sacred mystery together, anticipating his departure with the same awe with which one would look forward to a birth.

David stopped crying when I gave him the letter Charles had written. In it he apologized for not always having done the best for David and expressed his love for him. He said he would always love him and always watch over him. He also told David he "wanted him to have his photography equipment because he knew he could do beautiful things for God and man with it which would make his heart golden and full of joy." He wanted David to have his watch and ring and his tools when he was old enough, and whatever else "Mom would like you to have." David stopped crying when he finished the letter and ran out to the garage to look over some of the things Charles was going to leave him. David later wrote the following poem on the envelope of the letter: "Death itself is sometimes bad, but sometimes it is good, so be glad."

Friends invited David out regularly. He enjoyed the constant company and looked forward to different excursions.

The atmosphere was more intense on Charles's

last day. It was as though something else was in the
air. A friend had thoughtfully invited David to a late
movie. Charles's dad (he had been staying with us
for two weeks) went to sleep at nine-thirty P.M., anticipating early morning activity. I waited for David,
watched Charles breathe, and dozed. A favorite record kept playing over and over again. David got
home at twelve-thirty A.M. and went right to sleep.
Around two A.M. Charles's dad woke up. Charles was
gone.

David was very disappointed that I had not awak-
ened him when Charles died. I felt bad, too. I had
been glad that David was sound asleep during the
activities of the night, but I felt, in retrospect, it
would have been very meaningful for him. I wish
that he could have seen Charles when he first went.
He was very beautiful. He died serenely, with dignity. The atmosphere felt extremely peaceful and
full—as though the house was filled with the hosts of
heaven—a strong, sweet presence permeated the
room.

Plans Charles had made beforehand served to
prepare us for the moment. Charles had asked that
God's name be repeated for twenty-four hours and
that the remains and services be at home. He wanted
everything simple, joyous, honest, and from the
heart. No black. No minister. And anyone who
wished could say something.

David was very much a part of the funeral prepa-
rations. It was important to him. The saying of God's
name, the cleaning—everything.

We all felt upset when the remains were brought
back for the final gathering of friends. The life was
obviously no longer there and the body looked like a
mannequin. During the day David invited his friend
into the house to see his dad. I wondered what his

parents would think. Changes that occurred in the facial makeup upset David very much. During the entire day and into the evening, he kept going into the room to check on the body and would stand or sit for a while with his hands folded in prayer.

At the services David was very controlled. He would whisper to me, "I think I'm going to cry. Will you come in the other room with me?" And we would go into the other room and he would cry and then we would go back.

The day after the services, David and I drove up to the Bay Area with friends who had come down to help us. David didn't cry any more, but I was feeling the impact of our loss as if for the first time. When we finally arrived where we were to stay and David fell asleep, I cried through the night and into the next day. During the day David appeared matter-of-fact and would peek in at me and then report that I was still crying. I was embarrassed to have lost control and perhaps David felt similarly, but our friend was supportive. It was comforting when she told David, "Sometimes it's good to cry."

Ten months later we stayed with friends—a family. David felt close to the dad. On the way home he said, "I wish Dad were still here," and started to cry. It was as if it had registered afresh—Charles wasn't there anymore. David said it hurt in his chest. I was driving and felt stunned and at a loss for words. A friend who accompanied us suggested that David get in the front seat. He did and was comforted.

For a week after that occurrence, David grieved for Charles every night before he went to sleep. Then it passed.

We would never have chosen to go through a loss experience, but it brought the three of us together in a very deep and meaningful way and served to *con-*

nect us with the many others who so willingly and lovingly gave so much of themselves.

During a crisis one's emotional perception may become heightened—as though the heart, having been opened by pain, is enabled to feel life's loveliness with a newfound intensity. I don't know that I could have sustained an emotional life of that nature for long, nor that I personally transcended myself in any sacrificial acts of selfless service; but having gone through it, I do know that people are incredibly capable of reaching out to one another. Although I've long believed we are *all one,* the experience served to bridge theory with a tiny taste of actuality.

Words couldn't describe the gentle sweetness that seemed to emanate from Charles's very being. What better legacy could he have left us than mirroring the beauty of a perspective which seemed to transcend selfish desires and petty longings?

I can't say that my day-to-day activities reflect that glimpse of the loveliness I saw. It's easy to forget and get caught up in the struggle for self-supremacy and the quest for me and mine. But I do know a little, when I take the time to remember, that we're really just on loan for one another, that it's a moment-by-moment thing—and when I can catch myself between forgetting, I value the gift of my relationship with David in a very special way.

> In HIS time, we've got
>   FOREVER;
> But in the time we've been given,
>   we've got only
>   TODAY.

BROOKSIDE EMERGENCY ROOM—
FOR CAROL

your first born has been in a fever for a week
they keep you home with him in Vallejo
kneeling by his bed to catch the vomit
in a blue plastic pan
lest he aspirate
the second night he does not know you
the third you fall asleep across his comforter
the stench wakes you
so he does not suffocate
five nights up you ease him down on his side
he fights
flops over prone
so you curse him and flee
the sixth night at dinner a steak knife
punctures your palm
still they hold you in Vallejo to
wait out a virus
no point in wasting a teacher's pay
testing for TB or pneumonia
children don't get those now you
rush him to emergency at 105
you are delirious
a shadow on his left lung
strep pneumonia very rarely seen
in five year olds
two days to cure with wonder drugs
but what about the seven days lost rest
jagged palm
reeking hair
unwashed cannot stop the shrieking comes
with the territory mother's
prognosis uncertain.

                                    VICTORIA

NOTES

1. Summary of crisis theory, taken from the opening presentation at the Adolescents in Crisis Workshop by Paul W. Pretzel, Ph.D., Consultant, Los Angeles County Suicide Prevention Center. Based in part on work by Eric Lindemann, "The Meaning of Crisis in Individual and Family Living," *Teachers College Record* (1957), pp. 57, 310, 315.
2. James Coleman, *Abnormal Psychology and Modern Life* (Glenview, Ill.: Scott, Foresman and Company, 1976), pp. 171–72.
3. Pretzel summary.
4. James Coleman, *Abnormal Psychology*, p. 486.
5. Virginia Satir, *Conjoint Family Therapy* (Palo Alto, Calif.: Science and Behavior Books, Inc., 1969), p. 2.
6. Gerald Caplan, *Approach to Community Mental Health*, pp. 80–81.
7. Meher Baba, *Listen Humanity*, narrated and edited by D. E. Stevens (New York: Dodd, Mead & Company, 1957).

7. Articulating Our Thoughts and Dreams

October 17, 1976:

I finally washed the kitchen floor at 10 P.M. just so I could tell myself something was done today. I never do get the corners clean or erase the streaks, or perhaps I haven't the patience to do it right. Sometimes it seems that everything I do is halfhearted: my cleaning, my mothering, this writing. Sometimes I see those other mothers with their organized diaper bags and their neatly packed picnic lunches on the way to baby gym, then getting their kids home for a prompt hot lunch and a nap, and ask, "Is that what it will be like when I'm a real mother?" . . .

November 5, 1976:

Today I feel good about my small talents, the children smiling around me, absorbing my energy. And I inhale theirs deeply, enthralled by their willingness to be pleased by me, to join me in my play.

This is an excerpt from one woman's notebook that she has kept more or less regularly and has seldom shared with anyone. The idea of keeping a journal describing her experiences as a parent came out of an innovative and well-received course, "How to Survive Motherhood." The aim of this course, taught by a mother of two young children, is not to detail the "shoulds" and "should nots" or to give general philosophical directives from a position

of expertise. The expressed goal of this class is to expose
mothers to parenting through a variety of sources, ranging
from traditional literature on the subject, the how-tos of
the field, to contemporary fiction and the wealth of
women's poetry on the subject of motherhood.

Parents in this course are encouraged to keep notebooks
of their dreams and thoughts about their daily lives for the
duration of the class. They are not necessarily asked to
share aloud what they write for themselves, but if they
do, what they have to say is given the same concentrated
attention as writing that has been bound and covered in
glossy paper.

What comes out of these writings and drawings? Our
interest here is not to make an aesthetic examination or
judgment of these finished products, but rather to examine the function they play in the course of defining ourselves in the parenting role.

EXCHANGE

When his seed was planted in my restless womb
All the magic flew out into the fog.

I never knew them again:
the sorrow or the melancholy dreams,
the beating wings or moth's fluttering.

These leaden mornings
we rock together in uneasy stillness.
Those lullabies I hummed tunelessly
when he nested within are silenced,
drowned out by the droning and the jingling.

It seems we must always exchange one gift
for another—
fertile dreams for conception, passion for birth.[1]

ANONYMOUS

This poem was written by a mother at a critical period of transition in her own growth. She had spent her entire pregnancy and the first year of her child's life studying and modeling herself after multiple parental molds, discarding one after another as they did not fit her. The contradictory examples, "the droning and jingling" around and within her, made it seem impossible to take a positive grip on her own directives for herself and her family.

In the writing of one short, simple poem, scribbled on a piece of paper in an old notebook and tucked in a desk drawer as soon as it was given form, she articulated a previously unvoiced response to this frustrating time in her life. For this mother, the process of finally putting into words—giving vent to a bottleneck of emotions—helped unblock her path. She was increasingly able to examine and clarify, to see where her true goals separated themselves from what she thought was expected from her. Writing down her thoughts made them real for her and invested them with the same power had by all those other words of advice she had read in the previous months. She chose a pen, but a parent can take up other tools: paintbrush, camera, even modeling clay, and use them well.

It's the process, not the product

"As we watch children in the nursery school, we may become more aware of the avenues of expression through art which are open to adults. In the nursery school, we see children expressing a feeling through an art medium. But the need for expression and the values of expression may be as great for us adults."[2]

Adults often hesitate to take up the tools for self-expression because somewhere along the line they decide that they don't use words fluently or draw properly. They tend to think of creative expression only in terms of the quality of the finished work and then stop themselves before they have even begun. "The anxious attention on the product rather than the process, the coloring books and other 'patterns' that were imposed on us all have served pretty effectively to prevent most of us from expressing ourselves through art."[3]

Katherine Read, in her text *The Nursery School: Human Relationships and Learning,* makes the connection between a contemporary approach to children's art now widely accepted among early childhood educators: that art for young children is primarily an outlet for feeling—an essential process for fulfillment and increased awareness—and our parallel needs as adults. By looking at the function of art in the growth of children, we can put in perspective the self-conscious prohibitions we have placed on our own creativity.

Until recently it was not uncommon for parents to disregard their child's early artwork, those first scribblings and blobs of bright paint, until they began producing realistic images: a stick figure or a recognizable tree. And at a young age children were already having their work compared with the "best" artist in their class. Our children will have the advantage of our more relaxed attitudes and our new awareness that those first attempts to cover a paper with color are just as important—and just as gratifying to a child—as the later masterpieces. We share their delight in the spontaneous process, not the masterful products of their creative efforts. We will benefit by extending our understanding and appreciation of children's art to our attempts to translate our experiences on paper.

Read emphasizes the importance of safeguarding children's use of art media as a vehicle for self-expression. She offers one firm rule: patterning, the making or setting of models, is strictly forbidden if we are to allow children maximum experimentation and growth from their art experience. The moment we impose "shoulds" and "should nots," simply on the basis of our adult examples, we have risked limiting their freedom of expression and diminished their ability to create their own symbols.

If we take these basic guidelines for children's creativity for our own, we, too, can free ourselves from a good deal of anxiety. We will give ourselves more room to grow by avoiding patterning our parenting roles after *fixed* models —from books, from films and television, from some conglomerate picture—or appraising our children in terms of what we think the ideal child should be.

We need to concentrate less on studying how to raise the brightest children or become the most efficient parents, and more on working with our relationship with each of our children and its particular ebb and flow. We need to give ourselves permission to try new ways of raising our children and in turn raising ourselves. If we do, we can clean our inner lens, see and record our children *as they are,* aware of the broad outlines for child development, knowledgeable about typical growth and behavior at certain ages, but still able to focus our main attention on the uniqueness of our children and our own values and goals. Taking the time to observe and acknowledge what is happening within us and in our families can give us both a precious document and a valuable map for growth.

Interviews

Keeping a journal

Excerpts from the diary of Dori Draper, 1970–71:

Symi, Greece, 1970— . . . I become bigger each day. I worried in the beginning that I wasn't really pregnant, kept waiting for definite signs. Finally, in my fourth month, Dr. Apostolides convinced me that there was actually a baby in there. I was delighted when the baby started kicking—such positive reassurance—in the sixth month; the real "action" began, and the baby's kicking became a major entertainment for Tom and me. . . .

. . . it's late, midnight. The sea is madly calling out to the night, rushing against the rocks, as if in defiance of being kept at bay all day. My baby, too, cries out to me. It is impatient to see the world. I know it . . . I feel it. . . .

. . . It is wonderful being "with child" in Greece. One is expected to do nothing but be and be happy. If one denies herself anything, the results may be catastrophic. Papa Tsingos (the priest) swore to me that one woman who was too shy to ask for a bite of food (which she smelled and wanted) went home and died. . . .

England . . . it is seven weeks before Aaron Mark or Sarah Elena arrives. I'm breathing and relaxing and getting more and more excited and scared. (Note: Sarah was born seven days after this entry—prematurely. Sarah and I remained in the hospital for six weeks—until she weighed five pounds.) . . . My moments of joy with Sarah began when I was alone with her for the first time. It shocked me to be with her, this new person whom I had known, but not known, for so long, as a kicking creature inside me. She and I were there together. I sat down on the bed and cried. She lay in her little bed, so tiny, perfect, beautiful. The days and weeks passed and I continued to be overjoyed and surprised when I saw her. But nothing could compare with the joy of that revelation when she and I were alone for the first time.

Lindos, Greece . . . Sarah is seven months old. She is happiness itself . . . so much love and joy in her beautiful little body—and how generous she is with her gifts. I am, every minute of the day, captivated by and aware of my intense love for her. . . . Can there be a more powerful human experience?

Berkeley, California, 1977—Sarah is six years old now. She is still a small, delicate child. I adore her, identify very strongly with her, and have tended to be overprotective. I've just recently realized that it's not so much Sarah who needs protecting, but rather the small child in myself. Sarah is doing fine; she is a joyful, lovely, creative, free spirit. But the child in me is crying out for love, for nurturing . . . and I must give it the same care that I've given Sarah, I must let my own inner child play and be free. . . .

For if I repress my own needs for happiness, self-fulfillment, and privacy, I fear that this great love will turn to resentment and anger on both our parts, and instead of developing strength and producing joy, this love will breed guilt, dependence, and more anger. . . . It is the story of so many parents and children. . . . I don't want this to happen to us. I'm determined that it won't.

Joan:

I remember how struck I was by how independent Emily had become. She seemed to need me so little. When we went to the circus and saw some friends, she climbed right into their laps. They even commented about how open and trusting she was. I looked at her with admiration, not sadness for the little baby who was moving away.

I write poems about my children as a documentation of my feelings about them and about me. Writing is a method of having some tangible continuity. The stages of their lives are fleeting, so having them down on paper is a way of making these moments real for myself and a future gift for them. They might know more about who I was to them as a mother all the way along.

I wrote often about my children when they were tiny, and less as they are getting older. I guess it takes periods when you have a lot going on to cause the poetry to flow. Things are at a balance with them right now.

ON HER OWN

Less of me than through me,
resting nine months in my womb,
she chose the birthdate of her namesake
to be born.

I gave a push.
She headed forward.

Now my child toddles in all directions,
extending to the arms of strangers,
deadweight of trust in their laps.

She is nourished by the love of others,
richer than my mother's milk.
(Her head never turned back
when my breast was gone.)

I stand in her shadow,
my arms stretched womb big and round
should she again seek my body
as her resting place.

JOAN ALEXANDER WEINSTEIN
May 1976

Lorraine, age 28; boy, age 10, girl, age 4:
I always wanted a lot of kids; my grandmother had eleven children and I liked that feeling I got around a

big family. But I wouldn't want a large family now. Society has changed; conditions seem so bad—the world is changing, people getting hurt, not getting jobs, not enough money.

I didn't really feel like a mother for a long time. I was a senior in high school when he was born, so my mother cared for him, fed him, bathed him. The first nine or so months of his life, I didn't have responsibility for him. I guess I didn't feel like the mother of a baby until I gave birth to my second child. . . .

I was in a creative writing class in school when my first child was little, and I was writing all the time. My teacher thought I should go on to college and major in writing. I didn't want to do that, but I did like to write, to get my personal feelings down. I wrote so I could read it for myself.

The poem for my son came to me when I thought about things happening to him that I could remember in myself. I had little flashes of what being young felt like, the hurts. . . .

LONELINESS, GAMES, AND ME

Lonely and lost
A game I played when I was a child
I reached out for my mother's breast
When I got thirsty
I roved the ground for dirt to eat
When I got hungry
The slightest pain I felt
I ran home to mommy
When I got teased or embarrassed
When money played the game
I sat on daddy's lap
Sorrow deep down within my eyes
He smiled and gave

I watch children play now
My size, my age, my son
I see death come with days and time
I watch moments pass by with birth
I clutch to my child
Starved
To protect him from
Burdens we laid down
Lonely and lost am I
A game still played deep within
Nestled among, mind and thoughts
Buried behind reality
To face Nothing, stillness and ME

LORRAINE BESS

Marti:

This poem was written at a particularly trying time
for my four-year-old son and myself. He was having
a hard time at nursery school. Everything seemed to
frustrate him, and he wasn't able to slow down long
enough to learn some of the steps that would help
him along. He wanted to climb a tree, he wanted to
ride a bike, he wanted to make "real things."

Watching him go through these trials was very
distressing. One of his teachers commented that he
was moody. "He certainly has his ups and downs,"
she said. I took this statement as a judgment about
him and also about the way I was handling him. In
retrospect, I can see she meant he had mood swings
like any other four-year-old. Writing this poem was a
way of describing for myself how I saw my child at
that moment and of affirming how special he was.

HE HAS HIS UPS AND DOWNS

You ride the days
up and down,
dark-rimmed brown eyes
taking in the broad outlines,
small details,
the twists and flaws and
juice spills
without censoring.

All gallop,
no trot,
you haven't learned to jump the ditches,
seek out soft pastures,
so you take the jolts to heart.

You cannot ride them out, but make your own storms,
in the crowd of sunny children blessed with
                              tunnel vision.

                              MARTI
                              December 1975

Judy:
Writing the following poem helped me to understand
what I had really wanted from my mother: freedom
to grow and to be myself along with a strong sense
of security in being cared for and loved. Once I knew
this I realized that it was now up to me to be this
kind of mother to myself. I needed to try to be more
loving, accepting, and nurturing to myself.

The process of parenting myself requires changing
attitudes that run very deep. It takes time and
patience, but the rewards are great. As I begin to
give myself this mothering, I find that I quite nat-

urally begin to parent my children in a similar fashion.

Mother,
My spirit is a kite.
I long to fly ever higher
into blue beyondness.
But keep a firm hand on my string, please.
Let it unwind in favorable winds;
Take up the slack when the wind dies down
And never forget to reel me in
When nightfall or stormy weather comes.

JUDY PHILLIPS

Helane:

My daughter was so much more in tune with nature than I was. She was teaching me the cycle of life, which is the beautiful gift of being a mother—roles get reversed and sometimes she is my teacher. I just wanted to record this sharing as a moment of integrity and beauty.

SPRING GARDEN

She weeds my winter's lethargy
Like dandelions she calls fairies
Growing between the marigolds and snapdragons.
She says it's time to sow some seeds
And finds a clearing by winter's lettuce
        gone to seed.
With watering can and sand shovel
She sets to work
Proclaiming it our spring garden,
She a bud of five herself.

I could have left my earth unturned,
     my garden fallow,
And slumbered through another season,
I wouldn't have minded that.
But she sensed that spring had come
And my winter's thicket overgrown
And she had not wakened me
And had I slept 'til summer,
I could not nurture my precious bud,
Now blooming and opening fresh petals
     to the sun.

          HELANE ZEIGER
          1976

BRIGHT BABY (A LULLABY)

bright baby—bright baby
let me sing you a tune
of summer turning softly
on rocking-horse moons.
bright baby—bright baby
my hair still winds long
where is the proud love
that shares this sweet song?

on waves made of ivory
with elephant-fish
that dance on a thistle
and grant your third wish.

oh—one is for people
and two's for the show
the third is for lovers
with no place to go.

oh the people will flourish
and all will flow by

so—bright baby—bright baby
you don't have to cry.

GAIL SHAFARMAN

Gail:

I wrote this when Elyse was three months old. I wanted to give her a gift in rhyme. It has a slightly bittersweet tone, and that was what I felt then. A tinge of sadness, and recognition of growth through experiencing these emotions. I was coming to terms with a new role for myself, a need to explore where I was as a young woman.

There's a part of me that wants to make life perfect for my daughter, but I know I can't protect her, I need to allow her to go out and experience pain and sickness. Being a mother is not magical; this poem was a way of expressing my recognition of her right to live her own life.

TO ELYSE—AT THREE MONTHS (A POEM FRAGMENT)

my child—how can i see you
through the webs of the world
there are so many things
that flow away from us.
i cannot change the patterns
of our lives
or twist to desire
the shadows that must be.
    clear-eyed infant
    you play fearlessly with time
    and give yourself completely
    to the ever-changing day.

GAIL SHAFARMAN

This poem is intentionally sentimental, a recognition of my love for her, how beautiful her being eight was for me. If at future times we have difficulties, this poem will stand for what it was. It won't change the course of our future, it won't spare us what pain might lie ahead in our relationship. It will be there for us to remind us of what her being eight with me as her mother was.

TO ELYSE—AT EIGHT

i want you to know about immediate pleasure
what you mean to me
right now.
the pleasure of your beauty
so fine and careless
lithe—like the animals
you consistently admire.
and the clearness of your love
so guileless—it shocks
and i am tender kindling to its flame.
there is much to be learned
of complexity
and the cold caress
of human life.
and yet—
unexpectedly in the morning
you travel through silent
half-formed dreams
to waken.
and i tremble
when i greet you.

GAIL SHAFARMAN

Gail:

I wrote this story after I was sick and my daughter had gone through a hard time, developing an attachment to a stuffed animal. It upset me that she needed to find a substitute for my full attention and affection, since when I was sick I did not have much energy for her. I resolved some things for myself by writing this, and wanted to share what I was finding with other mothers and their children.

WHERE'S PRIM?

. . . Prim and Jennifer curled up tight in a baby ball together and got extra Daddy kisses. "Mommy's feeling better," whispered Daddy when he said good night.

Two hours later, Jennifer woke up alone in her bed. It was very dark. Where was Prim? Prim was gone. For good. "Mommy-Daddy-Prim—Mommy-Mommy," she called. Jennifer was so scared she couldn't move. Someone turned on the lights. It was Mommy. She didn't look too sick. "Come sit in my lap," she said, and scooped up Jennifer quickly in her arms. They sat tight and quiet for a few minutes. Then Mommy began to talk. "I want you to listen with the big girl part of you. I want the four-year-old Jennifer to hear. I know the past few weeks have been hard. Maybe you've been scared or afraid or lonely even with Daddy at home. I know that I've felt sad and I wanted to be with you very much. But I couldn't stop being sick. There are some things that even Mommies can't change. But I have a secret to share with you, Jennifer. I've already met Prim. Not the yarn bunny that you love, but the inside Prim that's part of you. I know her. She's the little one that likes warm milk and lots of snuggles. You can never lose her. She's with you for life, and I love her just like I love my big girl close in my lap. So you don't have to be scared anymore." Jennifer felt very safe and happy. "Can we find my bunny Prim now, please?" she asked. "Yes," said Mommy. So they turned down the blankets together, and there inside the flowered quilt was Prim, rumpled, graying, and beautiful. "It's bath time for both of you in the morning," said Mommy, as she tucked them into bed. They slept for a long, long time.

A letter Susan wrote:

Dear Matthew and Gabrielle,

You have made me a mother and yet ironically you will probably never know what mothering meant to me. You will always see me through the eyes of your own evolving experience and that's how it should be. Although that may not be true. I remember right after you were born, Matthew and Gabrielle, I was struck so with the overwhelming intensity of my feelings for you that I paused to think—is this what my mother once felt for me? For a moment I stepped out of my childhood mythology. I was awed and I was grateful. Maybe some day that will happen to you but I won't count on it. Mostly because I experience my everyday life with you as its own reward—a substance that changes shape constantly before my eyes.

For years I imagined you . . . just as you are now, Gabrielle, even as you run, headlong, at every baby you see and and nurture your dolls with infinite care. It was as if you were created inside of me—more by imagination than any physical process. But that imagination was like nighttime dreams compared with the reality of the spiritual force that moved through me and brought you into my keeping.

Some people say once a mother always a mother. This is often to justify the maternal feeling that accompanies their relationship with their children into adulthood. But for you, M and G, I have already been many mothers, and you have taught me to relinquish some of them as you emerge and ask me to grow with you. I really have no choice. If I remain the mother who wants to hold you in my arms and be your only comfort, you will fire me. You will find reinforcement for your independence elsewhere. But the "infant mother" is still inside me as well as the mother who followed you down a San Francisco street when you toddled up every staircase you could find. What am I to do with these mothers? Shall I file them on the shelf for another baby along with your outgrown clothes? Or should I let them out of the closet covertly when you are tired and are not armored against their presence.

I experience these identities as a problem. They do not want to go away. And maybe the new mothers that you demand do not want to come out. But you draw them, like a snake charmer with the realities of your growth, and leave me to fight my multi-identity problem on a level within. And they are my problem. I find as you grow that I can become more of the person I was before you were born, or maybe a continuation of that person. Your companion on the path. And you seem to like me. This person is not a mother; that was and is just one phase along the journey. So maybe this person is the one you will finally know, because she will outgrow each of the roles she chooses and is required to fill.

But some day, dear ones, I hope you remember the mother. She will seem very young to you then. You won't remember her when she had dark hair untouched by gray or soft skin unwrinkled and smooth for you to sleep upon. She will amaze you in photographs because she doesn't exist in your conscious life.

But some day when you hold a baby, maybe it will not even be your own, I hope that far memory reaches you and you stand in awe of your feelings and permit again the realization of what I will always feel for you.

In His love,
Susan

NOTES

1. Shakespeare's Sisters, eds., *If We Know Where the Poems Come from, Why Don't We Just Go There* (San Lorenzo, Calif.: Shameless Hussy Press, 1976), p. 7.
2. Katherine Read, *The Nursery School: Human Relationships and Learning* (Philadelphia: W. B. Saunders Co., 1976), p. 261.
3. *Ibid.*, p. 269.

8. Clarifying Our Values

One area that concerns parents is the many and often conflicting values in our society that continually bombard children. These values come from t.v., travel, new and different neighbors and schoolmates and other sources. In a simpler society, children grew up with an entire community espousing the same basic values concerning such subjects as religion, sex, work, responsibility, and education. One of the most widely discussed subjects today, drugs, was not even heard of, or heard of only vaguely. Think now of the many choices a junior high school student has to make today.[1]

Children grow up behaving well and responsibly primarily because they love their parents who have loved them. They want to please their parents most of the time and be like them. But, for this system to work well, the parents must have ideals of one kind or another. They have to know what they expect of their children and communicate this to them clearly.[2]

Why do I approve or disapprove of this suggestion or option? Is it because my own parents would have behaved this way? Is it because of what others might think? Is it because of some childish fear in myself? Or after looking over all the facts, I believe that this option, perhaps suggested by the child, is really reasonable (or unreasonable)? We want to base our judgment, as much as possible, on this last statement rather than any of the others.[3]

Can you imagine yourself looking back in eighteen years?
. . . the exchange between husband and wife about the children—talks far into the night—builds your courage and how you handled certain problems. Talking this out, with the child or between yourselves, helps expose both sides of the question. You will see how groundless many worries are and how hugely funny certain situations are, which don't seem at all amusing at the time. And finally, you will come to the conclusion that you cannot change a child, you can only guide her.[4]

Problems

1. A mother and her twelve-year-old daughter live alone and have managed to keep a very open relationship. They discuss sex, drugs, and other issues that other families may find off limits. When the daughter comes home and relates the fact that the average age of intercourse for girls in the United States is fourteen, according to her junior high teacher, and asks if she can get birth control pills when she reaches that age, the mother feels conflicted.

2. A low-income black mother feels dismayed that her three-year-old son is not being taught to read in preschool. She feels with all the publicity on ghetto children being behind in the three *R*'s that his young white teacher's failure to provide these basics may result in later school failure.

3. A father finds that taking his four-year-old daughter shopping is a constant battle. She insists on buying all the junk food she sees on TV commercials, and when he talks to her about good nutrition, she argues that everyone else in the neighborhood gets these treats. A little less than half the time she wins.

4. A Native American family living in a predominantly white community is angered when the school sends home material for their child to join the Mexican-American bilingual program. They want their child to have a strong

cultural identity and resent the fact that the teacher has never bothered to find out about the child's background and is just assuming he is Mexican.

5. A young divorced mother feels that she needs to have relationships with men but wonders how to handle sexuality in view of the model she has to set for her eleven-year-old daughter.

6. A mother worries that her child won't have friends if she insists that he cannot watch TV at his friends' houses where daytime TV is allowed.

7. A sixteen-year-old boy's parents question their son's decision when he says that he wants to transfer to a non-academic high school rather than continue in his college-prep class.

At a time when we are used to hearing about the most dire family crises, these situations may seem a little tame and unsensational. However, most of the decisions we make in everyday life are like these—not earthshaking, but challenging. The little decisions can be rather provocative because what we decide, and how we communicate it, has consequences for our relationships, and those little choices make up a pattern that helps to shape the course of our lives.

In these examples we have given you only outlines and we would like you to fill in the rest. How do you think the parents in these examples feel? What are their conflicts? What beliefs or values might they hold? What might be the other forces influencing their children's lives? What are the options for these families? What are the best ways of reaching their decisions? What might be the consequences of some of their choices?

If you take the time to fill in these sketches with your own perceptions and backgrounds, you may discover that what you have is not a series of unrelated situations but an image of a dynamic process. Parents at work. People defining what's important to them, meeting situations that force them to turn one way or another, or ignoring the process altogether.

Most of us are not lucky enough to have been given definitive instruction on how to engage creatively in this process. If you were born within the last twenty years, you may have had some training in junior high or high school in what is currently called the values clarification approach. Within the last decade, some of you may have attended a workshop on the subject of values. With change and diversity working like an epidemic to breed confusion in our society, some psychologists felt it was important to develop techniques to help people clarify where they stand, what they believe. The values clarification approach was developed to fill the vacuum created by the destruction of fixed values. It's an approach designed to help us make sense of the world and the overwhelming choices we all have to make.

The main thrust of the values clarification approach has been aimed at youth at a very vulnerable and critical stage in their social and moral development. It is designed to help them make effective choices among all the possibilities they have available. Unfortunately, very little values clarification work has been done specifically with parents. This is ironic when you consider the number of decisions a parent has to make in the course of child rearing.

The crises of youth might be expressed by these questions: Who am I? Who do I want to be? What might the consequences be of some of the options I am offered now? How can I affect the world around me?

The crises of parenthood contain all those questions that come and go throughout our lives with varying intensity. In addition, parents feel the weight of moral responsibility for their children and what they might become. The question many parents ask is, If I have a picture of the type of adult I would like my child to become, do I know how or have the right to try to make him conform to it?

Many people living in these times of a relativistic "do

your own thing" philosophy would answer the last question with an unequivocal no. Parents have been admonished for stuffing their own values down their children's throats. But they have also been condemned for not having taught them "proper values," that is, manners and respect, when their children display what people consider inappropriate behavior. Not enough attention has been given to helping parents sort out conflicts about their values and the ways they relate to a changing society.

In the examples outlined, there are controversies we are all familiar with, even if we have not experienced them in our own lives. There is controversy over the role of schools versus the home in discipline and authority; over the effects of television and peer culture on the values and models that our children adopt; over the overwhelming choices presented to adolescents; over the problems of subcultures and their diverse value systems as related to the dominant society; over our own changing values and their effects on our children.

These are everyday dilemmas that do not necessarily lead to crisis. Often we let them glide by us, feeling that they are not important enough or that we do not have options or choices enough to give them much attention. How many parents have examined such issues so thoroughly that they have sorted out their attitudes and established goals for their own behavior?

One father writes:

The family must seize responsibility back from the government, from industry, from the schools, from society at large. The family must reclaim its functions.

To do anything else is both cowardly and unwise. It is cowardly because it means evading one's personal responsibilities. Parents neither deserve respect nor respect themselves when they are aware just off the edge of their consciousness that they are evading responsibilities. It is unwise because one can see with one's own eyes that neither the state nor the dominant culture has proven to be morally trustworthy.

There is much talk nowadays about "creativity" in the family. The primary act of creation in the family, however, is to create a way of life, a tiny, modest, moral cosmos. "This is how we wish to live our lives," a family in effect tells the world. "Do your worst, world, here we stand."⁵

Is it possible to create our own moral universe? Michael Novak, the philosopher-father who wrote this quote, has obviously thought through his values—measured them against those held by others in this society and found some conflicts.

The picture he has of the role of the family vis-à-vis society may not be our picture, but the question here is, Do we have any picture at all of what we want and what values we want our children to develop, to hold? Most of us do not take such an absolute stance. We more often raise our children through day-to-day practicalities guided by vague notions of what is or isn't right or true. Whether we agree with Mr. Novak or not, he makes a strong point; the family has a responsibility, he insists, to "create a way of life" based on its own perception of truth. That creativity, which he feels is the essence of family life, requires examination of the beliefs that we express in our everyday actions.

If we fail to accept this responsibility, maybe it is because of another conflicting value that we hold dear, rather than an abdication of responsibility, as Novak suggests. What lies at the bottom of many of our decisions or lack of decisions on conflicted values is the strong belief that we don't want our children to be different. We want them to fit in, to be popular, to have friends. This attitude is so deep and pervasive in our society that we often overlook it.

The woman who has worried about her son not having friends because he is not allowed to watch TV is the mother of a three-year-old. We might ask ourselves in what other cultures or at what other time in history has the peer group of a three-year-old been so important that we have to worry about this early ostracism. And yet we are terrified of the peer group and its influence as children grow older—never stopping to think that our own underlying values and assumptions about popularity have helped give this outside sphere its power. And so we are caught over and over again in seemingly insolvable conflicts, often because of our own underlying value conflicts and our inability to see the way they influence our perceptions. It is easy and comfortable to say that society and its lack of morality is ruining our children. It is perhaps more productive to look at the way some of our own attitudes are a part of our society's problems, so that we can contribute to the solutions. And it all comes back to a question of values and our awareness of them.

What do we need in order to look at these values? The descriptions, predictions, and prescriptions of social scientists and psychologists can seem downright depressing.

In his book *Two Worlds of Childhood*, Urie Bronfenbrenner, the well-known social and developmental psychologist, compares American and Soviet families, looking at some of the influences and possible effects of childrearing patterns. He talks about the "unmaking of the American child," who is so much more prone to antisocial behavior than his Soviet counterpart. He points to the lack of contact in American families, the influence of TV, the lack of involvement of American parents in guiding their young. "England is . . . the only country which shows a level of parental involvement lower than our own, with both parents—and especially fathers—showing less affection, offering less companionship, and intervening less frequently in the lives of children."[6] He sees TV and the peer group as primary influences on the values of children in America.

What are the reasons for this lack of guidance and lack of involvement? On the part of American parents, in most cases, it isn't lack of concern. And, in fact, most parents have strong ideals. We can point to social problems as the roots of the confusion over our values and our inability to communicate them, but it's hard to say which came first. It may be more constructive to look at values such as individualism, consumerism, and mobility and see how they influence our child-rearing patterns and life-styles.

In his book *Let Our Children Go!*, Ted Patrick argues that the underlying values of a culture can contribute to the growth of and ignoring of a social problem. In his examination of many of the youth cults, he reports violence, crime, and social ills, which he feels society permits *because* of our strong convictions about religious freedom and noninterference in religious activity. Whether his perceptions or methods are valid is another question of values, but his analysis provides provocative material that no parent can afford to ignore.

Have we abdicated the responsibility of exploring values with our children without even knowing it? And if we have, how is that abdication reflected in the social problems we are now facing?

Whether we have abdicated or just been ineffectual at it, the critical issue is, Where do we go from here? Should we become stronger in moralizing about our values to our children at a younger and younger age? Should we provide stronger models for them, hoping they will follow our own example more willingly than our words? Should we let them find their own values without our interference? There are intervening factors that make any of these processes ineffective in themselves. Children are presented with such a diversity of influences and models today that any of these approaches leaves young people vulnerable to forces we would have them be armed against.

Another approach that is described in the book *Values Clarification* by Simon, Howe, and Kirschenbaum is concerned not with inculcating values but with exploring their content and sources through a dynamic process. The focus is on how people come to hold certain beliefs and follow certain behavior patterns. The authors say it is not a new approach because there have always been parents and teachers who have examined and helped others to examine their values and decisions. However, the values clarification approach is more systematic. The book outlines seven substeps crucial to the process of valuing:[7]

Prizing one's beliefs and behaviors:
1. Prizing and cherishing
2. Publicly affirming when appropriate
3. Choosing from alternatives
4. Choosing after consideration of consequences
5. Choosing freely

Acting on one's beliefs:
6. Acting
7. Acting with a pattern, consistency, and repetition

Obviously this system is not only an analytical but an actualizing one. A person has to perform all of the substeps to check if a notion is something that is informing his life and is therefore a value, not a goal or an attitude.

Since this process can be engaged in individually or with others, we can discover what we believe and act on in the context of what others around us believe and do. We can use this process to engage our children in talking about how they feel about things that happen to them at home and at school. We can help them to think through situations, information, and decisions critically by encouraging open discussion and teaching them about the process of valuing.

However, it would be a mistake to think that teaching our children to clarify their values is enough. We also have to become aware of the way our own decisions and behavior—about food, play, discipline, learning, education, relationships—reflect our view of life and what we think a human being should be. We have to develop our abilities to talk about what we believe.

Unless parents are very young, discovering our values is not usually complex and may seem relatively easy and fun. The difficulty for parents seems to come in (1) deciding how to implement those values, (2) deciding the consequences of our actions, (3) understanding our values conflicts, and (4) being able to affirm our values publicly.

If you have looked, look again at the examples we have given and answer the questions; you will see that most of the problems do not derive from a parent's not having values or even not knowing what they are, but from a confusion over implementing those values in the face of other internal or external pressures. Looking at the examples, what are the values conflicts?

What are the problems in communicating those values?

Parents need to look at the origins of their beliefs and to determine which of them have been freely chosen with an awareness of other alternatives. They need to be willing to take the risk, to share their prized values and understand their values conflicts.

- A mother may want her daughter to be open enough to talk about wanting birth control pills but be opposed to the idea of giving her approval for her having sex. This is a valid stance but involves two values that may be in conflict with each other. They do not have to be mutually exclusive. Perhaps she has to have the courage to talk openly about these values with her daughter so that they can come together to some kind of resolution, before a lack of communication or actual circumstances set off a crisis.

· A father may enjoy watching TV himself as a form of relaxation but abhor some of the effects he sees and reads it has on his child.

If we see that we can, and often do, have conflicting desires and beliefs even within ourselves, we can start to examine which of those is a value we want to abide by in a specific situation at a specific time. It is this examination that helps us to live with our decisions and publicly affirm them to others. Seeing our own conflicts can also help us to understand that the behavior of others is not necessarily wrong but based possibly on different beliefs, different perspectives.

When a neighbor or a close friend comes over and her children jump on our furniture and leave out all the toys—behavior we don't allow our children—being willing to discuss our values can help us to deal with the situation in a constructive manner. Often such an incident results in an all-or-nothing attitude—either to put up with behavior we dislike or terminate the relationship. Neither are really necessary if we are willing to look at and explore other options.

It is impossible to go through life today without values conflicts, even if we don't deal with them. It is important to practice the art of recognizing them and handling them creatively. This does not always mean that we have to have a direct confrontation. We can learn to be tactful but consistent about our beliefs without alienating others. Many people change their attitudes through communication with people they have learned to respect. If we discuss our values and learn to implement them with some consistency, we can open ourselves to the flexible stance of being influential and influenced by others.

Most values conflicts occur at home. Husbands and wives inevitably have some different interests and beliefs, even if they were raised next door to each other. It would be impossible for two people to agree on everything or even most things (just consider our divorce rate), so the important question is the process by which these values conflicts are resolved. By viewing our values as a process, we can give up the more limiting stance of having to decide who is right and who is wrong.

Single parents who share their homes or live in alternative family systems often go their own ways because of different child-rearing styles or values. Learning to discuss what we prize and cherish with an attitude that allows the other person to have different values can broaden our views and lead to compromise and respect. On the playground, in the school, in religious settings, in public places, and in our own homes, we can never assume that even if we have goals similar to others, our ways of interpreting or implementing them will be the same.

Values out in the world

Our ability to articulate what we believe may be the very force that helps to change a teacher's attitude, a school's policies, a community's priorities, or to preserve our relationship with a friend.

With the subject of day care so current, the question of values may be at the center of the controversy. Quoting Michael Novak again: "Does anyone really think that 'child care professionals' could ever be paid enough to make them equal to mothers and fathers in caring, intuitive understanding, and long term consistency? Here is a values conflict that is at the very core of the day care controversy—who should raise the children? Who will do the best job?"[8]

This controversy may be valid but irrelevant, because regardless of who is most qualified to care for children, parents and children in our society need alternatives to in-the-home care. Perhaps it is parents' articulation of their goals and beliefs for their children that will enable day care workers to best extend the kind of care that complements the home. *Discussion of values is crucial.* Parents can learn to determine the best school or day care setting by asking questions that reveal the values of those who will teach their children.

This does not mean that we cannot tolerate diversity. We and our children can benefit from the diversity of values around us. A teacher does not have to treat a child or even see her the same way the parent does. She does not have to have the same goals for that child. But it is the ability of the teacher and parent to understand and respect each other's values that can act as a catalyst for making the relationships effective.

Perhaps in some very important ways the acute social problems that have affected our children and our families will in the end serve us well. As a start, they have broken down feelings of separation between classes and social groups—no parent can realistically say today, "That would never happen to my child." The lesson has been brought home over and over again too dearly. The same life-shaking conflicts—from drug abuse to divorce—now involve every segment of society. So we are forced to look at problems as relevant to us and to explore common solutions.

We are also forced to make decisions about the kind of life we want to lead. More and more parents are becoming conscious of the values and priorities in their lives and are making radical decisions such as not accepting job promotions in order to stay in the same neighborhood, moving out of the city to the country or the suburbs, and reassessing the schools their children attend. These decisions have, of course, been made in the past, but today more of them seem to be based on values that are not economic at the core. Our problems, if nothing else, will make us form new kinds of relationships with our children. We will have to take our own values seriously, especially the way we model and carry them out. We will have to become more involved in assessing the world with our children—helping them to make and explore choices—if we want the family to survive.

Friends, neighborhoods, and communities may form new coalitions based on common values and problems that help to develop or reinforce common beliefs. People with common interests about children are already starting to join together to lobby for governmental reinforcement of values in the areas of TV, day care, child abuse, pornography, and education. The more "grass roots" discussion of values that occurs, the more opportunity for social change.

If we approach valuing as a process, we will also be encouraged to look at our lives in the "here and now"—the values we are living today, how we are acting on them, how we are publicly affirming them, how we are articulating them and changing them—rather than working toward some ill-defined or even nonexistent goal. It does not guarantee that we won't go through the crises; only that we will be more aware in our understanding and handling of them.

As a person, parent, friend, spouse: Who am I? Where do I want to go from here? How does my life reflect what I believe? Maybe finally we can be thankful that these questions have been imposed on us. Maybe we would not choose to lead our lives creatively, unless that were one of our only alternatives. Nevertheless, by changing ourselves, we may usher in a new age.

Interviews

*There is always the question—what do I
believe about children?*

A feeling can become a value when we make a conscious
decision to make it so. Then we have to be willing to express it in our lives or change it when it no longer fits.

Gail:

We've had no difficulty with limits because we really
believe in them. I don't think it does a kid any good
to see that you have no needs yourself. I read enough
to know that I wasn't expecting too much at a particular level. Why should I expect an eighteen-month-
old to be content in a restaurant for two hours while I
eat? My expectation was that I would have to spend
time walking her around for some part of that meal
if I chose to take her with me. People used to say,
"Why don't you just let her scream?" I said, "I don't
think a child that age should be expected to stay put.
It will come." It wasn't appropriate to expect her to sit
that long, not then. I think I knew where I was coming from theoretically and held to it. On the other
hand, I have found it much more difficult than most
people to leave her. Everyone says, "Well, leave them,
they get used to it." But that's just not my philosophy. I consider mothering my full-time job, and I
just don't believe that. I deeply do not believe it will
be OK if I do that. I might see myself as being too
powerful. I think you do make a big difference in your
kid's life forever. It's just respecting her rights. She
has them, and we respect them, and it's got to go two
ways.

Q.: What are a baby's rights?

A.: I believe they deserve the very best in caretaking they can get.

Q.: What are your best qualities as a mother?

A.: Patience. I feel very confident. I have a belief system that I think works, so I believe in it and in myself. I feel my own ego is not involved in a power struggle. I remember what it is like to be a kid, very vividly. I think that's been a real asset.

Raising a teenager to make choices—how are values involved?

Our self-esteem is intimately involved with the courage we have to implement what we believe.

Linda, age 33, divorced; daughter, age 13:

I feel for the most part that my own parenting was very poor, but there were some very good parts. For instance—values. My parents taught me some very good values. Some were phony, I learned later. They were middle-class liberals but an awful lot of their liberalness was phony. Since I didn't know it was phony I took it to be the truth.

My parents said in words: money isn't important, don't build life around money. People are more important than money. In actions, I got the message—grab as much as you can get. Fortunately my own personal opinion, apart from theirs, is that money isn't very important to me. And I do feel people are more important. For the most part when I was growing up my parents had very little money. Dad was in school and we did without things that I wanted and needed. So I know how to do without things. As soon as Dad finished college he started making a lot of money. It seems that then their values changed from money is not important to let's buy everything in sight. But by that time my values were established. I believed what they had said.

Probably the most important value I learned from my parents was to value human beings. I probably learned that from my father. I was very close to him and respected him more than anyone in the world. My mother treated me very badly. He was the only adult friend I had, and I felt he respected me very much.

They left one extremely important value out which I had to learn the hard way. *That is to respect yourself.* I grew up with a terrible lack of self-esteem and self-worth. And I think it's one of the most important things you ever get.

I was absolutely thrilled out of my mind to be a mother. I've raised Nancy totally from my own instincts. I think I was born with them. I think they are part of me, the me that's separate from anyone else. I got all kinds of advice from my mother on what to do, but I didn't follow it always. For instance, Nancy was born in the winter and our house was cold. My mother told me you have to bathe a baby every day. I felt it wasn't necessary to bathe her every day. I kept her clean.

Nancy was born with congenital dislocated hips. We took her to General Hospital in Los Angeles and a team of experts took care of her from the time she was born. I always followed their advice. When she was four, they told me they thought she ought to have an operation on each hip so that she would never get arthritis. My mother told me not to let them do it. "They're butchers. She'll have terrible scars."

I used my own judgment. I felt that I'd rather take the advice of seven experts than hers. My mother died one year later and she never let up on me about the scars on Nancy; they are so faint you can hardly see them.

When she died I was totally free to follow whatever I thought without any interference. I think I have raised her unusually, compared to how other people raise their children.

She has tremendous self-respect, the value I wanted to get across the most to her. I don't know exactly why, except that I respect her very much. When I'm wrong I apologize. I don't feel afraid to change a decision that I've made. I appreciate her human beingness. I think very highly of her. I don't only love her, I like her very much.

Respect for other people's feelings has also been very important to me. I've stressed it all her life, and I've shown her the example of how I respect other people's feelings. A lot of people disagree with the way I raise her. I feel Nancy is entitled to express all her feelings to me. If she's angry she's entitled to yell.

Sometimes people feel it's wrong to give her the amount of information I do. Sometimes they're amazed. My daughter and I are very close. I don't want to be a hanging-on mother but sometimes it's hard to let go. When she is eighteen or nineteen, I want her to feel confident enough to handle life by herself and I'm practically positive she will.

It's very difficult sometimes to know what to let her do and what not to let her do. I trust her judgment about people. She's always had very good judgment about people. I check out the people she's associated with but I also trust her.

I have to make so many decisions all the time. If she tells me I'm unfair I think about it for a while. Sometimes we even try it her way and see how it works out. If it works out, fine; if it doesn't, I trust my instincts and say no. I tell her, "I know I don't own you." (She accuses me of thinking this.) "However, I'm responsible for you and until you're grown you just have to trust me. I'm not an unreasonable mother."

It's difficult to know when you are letting the reins go too much or when you're hanging on too much. Every decision is an individual thing. I just use my instincts and I think they're good.

On the problem of marijuana, I have told her it is a decision that will have to be hers. Practically everyone tries it, and I didn't want her to be afraid to tell me if she did. I didn't want her sneaking around. She hates drugs, won't go near it. I feel good without anything and so does she. I didn't want her to feel I would condemn her if she tried it. She made the decision herself.

She tests me every day just to see where Mama will draw the line. She came home one day with a glass of wine, which she had gotten from a neighbor, and showed it to me. I said, "Pour it out, people don't drink wine in the middle of the day." And she poured it out. She wants to see what I will permit. I won't permit that.

The testing is actually enjoyable because she's so cute. The thing I like most about her is she tells me everything. She comes home and says, "I don't want to talk about it." In a few minutes she says, "Aren't you going to ask me?"

Most of the decisions she tests me on I can make like that. Some are harder. She will ask if she can go out with so-and-so, he's only eighteen. I say no. She says she can handle everything. I say eighteen no, and explain why. Eighteen no, fourteen maybe.

I don't expect my child to be a super human being. She's not ready to go out with boys. She asks if she can go out with a boy who is a close friend. I say yes, but she never goes.

She has her own goals. She wants to be a marine biologist. She has since she was seven. She's planning to join the Coast Guard after high school. Then she wants to go to Scripps and study sharks and whales. That goal hasn't changed since she was eight. She doesn't say "if" I go to Scripps, she says "when." The GI Bill from the Coast Guard will pay for her to go.

She has a tremendous energy and a spark about her that makes me happy and proud I raised her. Not that I take credit, because she is who she is, but I think I brought out the best in her with my guidelines. Some parents feel it is dangerous to give a child information. I feel the opposite, that it is dangerous not to. I don't give other people's children information, but if they ask me a question I answer honestly. All Nancy's friends want to move in with me.

The religious question: recognizing different values and views

With the amount of ferment and change in religious circles themselves today, beliefs can become family-oriented issues, as exemplified in the next three interviews.

Alice, age 30, divorced; two girls, ages 8, 4:

My parents stressed one thing. And I don't. They were strict Catholics. They stressed observing the church laws. It was guilt-inducing because I discovered I was going through rituals not because of faith but because of my parents' demands. I don't know if they expected it or demanded. I never questioned. I suppose I'm reacting to what my parents did. I expose my children to religion by whatever they pick up naturally; that composes their religious education. I think religion is something you need to choose for yourself. The best Catholics are converts.

I try to spark an interest in them. There's not a

church that suits all my needs so I just do without a church. I handle moral teaching the same way my parents did though. They believed in teaching through example. The only time I really sit down and talk to my children about moral values is when someone, for example, lies. I try to point out, without judging that person, that lying could have been avoided, and how it wouldn't be right for my daughters to do the same thing.

I don't worry about the things they do now. But I think during adolescence I'll wonder if I've prepared them enough to make the right decisions. In some ways I wish they had more religious background, not Catholic. Friends who were Catholic went through a period of rebellion; when they came out of it they either had a good moral character or not. Some came out moral and others amoral.

Morality has to do with the way they treat their fellow man in my opinion. That's pretty much it, totally. If they treat them in a Christian way or not. People who are amoral have no conscience about treating them otherwise.

I wish they had more religious background, because I did and I'm not sure of the outcome for them. I don't want to cheat them.

Susie, age 34; three children, ages 8, 6, 3 months:
"Why don't children who go to church talk about Jesus instead of the devil?" my son asked repeatedly when we first moved into this churchgoing neighborhood from our old home. His question reflects a six-year-old's relentless attempts to make sense of the world and to rationalize the value system his parents have given him with that of the countless others he meets now in the world of school, neighborhood,

et cetera. This is a six-year-old's task. However, I think in our family some of this questioning has a slightly different flavor.

Most people in our country assume that if you are religious, you go to church or synagogue. When we first moved to this neighborhood, I felt on the first Sundays like our car, sitting in the driveway, standing out like a sore thumb. The view that spirituality and churchgoing are somehow synonymous is of course a naive one—but it is pervasive and can cause problems for a family who sees things in a different way. During a recent religious crusade, neighborhood children were paid to bring children who don't go to church to the meetings. My children wanted to go, not because they equated it with God, but because they wanted the prizes offered. When you're eight and six you also want to be like your friends and it's hard to have a spiritual view that few people in your new neighborhood have ever heard about. It is also true that comparing personal spiritual beliefs to the doctrines of organized religion is a complicated task even for an adult. It can be difficult when it has to start, as it does in many families, at an early age.

In our case, which is somewhat unique, we believe, in contrast to most of our neighbors, that the Saviour, or Avatar as we call him, has not come once but many times, in the persons of such universal figures as Zoroaster, Krishna, Buddha, Mohammed, Jesus, and most recently our own personal Master, Meher Baba, who lived in India until he died in 1969. Our children know the names of these men and something about most of their lives. They also know stories of saints, like Saint Francis, and before we came to our new neighborhood they knew nothing about the devil as a religious figure, but thought of him as a Hallowe'en character or a drawing on hams. We do not believe in the devil, and we also do not see God as someone cruel enough to sentence people to eternal damnation for the mistakes of one lifetime. We believe in reincarnation and life as a vast school where we work on individualized lessons which bring us closer to life's ultimate goal—union with God. We also work under a spiritual teacher—the only known teacher authorized by Meher Baba during his lifetime. Having a spiritual teacher is not something many people understand in our society except as it relates to the cults which currently receive so much publicity.

Ironically, our values are in some ways more like our devout Christian neighbors' than those of many of our atheist and agnostic friends. We have taken vows of one hundred percent honesty (my husband and myself), and we teach our children that honesty applies to *everything*, including things like giving back extra change that we got mistakenly and not making up excuses to tell someone if we don't want to go with them. However, even if we hold many of the Christian values, especially related to loving God and neighbor, we do not talk about our spiritual views unless asked. We do not try to distinguish ourselves in outward appearance or manner either. The fact of the matter is that if some of our neighbors knew what we believed they might denounce us as heretics. People often prefer atheistic views to those that say God has come again. We are both professionals and our colleagues know little of our personal views about religion, except what they observe in our behavior.

Many of our friends recoil at "laying their trips on their children." "We want them to choose for themselves," they say. In contrast, we impress our children with certain values quite heavily: honesty, love of God, being true to yourself rather than others. We don't want them to be left in a values vacuum where media, our views, the views of the kids on the playground all have equal weight. We see too many children floundering and making life-changing decisions too young. We don't believe our children will necessarily follow the same path we have chosen. We do feel that if they learn to love God, their strength and purpose of choice will follow.

Interestingly enough, they have learned discretion with their friends and in school without being told. "You know, Mom," my son said one day, "if I see a statue of Buddha when I'm with the other kids I don't say anything so they won't think I'm different." But he wonders why other children don't know about Buddha and Krishna. We talk about this a lot—about other people's values—in a way that we hope makes our children nonjudgmental but able to understand. It is this type of discrimination that we feel is crucial. That is why we don't simply say, "Don't do this, it's bad," but talk about how things we do fit in with what we want out of life—what we as a family are "trying to be." We hope this process of discussing will provide a model for their later decision making. We also hope it will make them tolerant of others. We feel that being somewhat at variance with the assumptions of the majority of people can help them to harmonize with others who have diverse values, and we see a depth of understanding developing in them even at this early age which we feel comes from discussing our view and how it fits into the world.

Connie, mother of three teenage children:

The church has been very important to our family life. If you take Christ and the power of God out—the spiritual benefits that you can't tell anyone about—just the social benefits are enough. There's a chance when a family is all by itself that it gets rotten, it develops strange ways of interacting, turns in on itself. But if you go once a week and just hear and interact with other people, it knocks some of the corners off—the hang-ups of just a mother and father raising children.

It's important to have one thing more important than anything. If God and the church is the important thing, then everything falls into line. Family and marriage have to be the result of God. If the family comes before that, the number-one thing, something funny happens. It's too changing.

Afro-American identity: a couple united in strong values and concern

The values of many subcultures in our society are in a state of radical change. A husband and wife having clear ideas on what they want for their children is the first step in implementing those individual and group values that they have chosen.

Starla Hollins is a counselor and teacher of Afro-American and African studies. She is twenty-seven and her husband, Larry, is twenty-six. They have a daughter, Aisha, who is five months old.

Starla:

We wanted a daughter. Actually I was neutral, but my husband wanted one so much that just before she was born I started wanting one. Every day he would play Stevie Wonder's song "Isn't She Lovely?" about his daughter. He wanted a little me. When the doctor said she was a girl, he started to cry and he said, "Oh, she's beautiful." When I got to hold her I was really high. When they took her away I cried. Then he declared his love for me. I wanted to keep her and keep her.

We're both into identity and self-concept. We've tossed around how we feel about what we want for her. When people say she looks like one of us we say she's the best of both of us—but she's really herself. We didn't name her for three weeks. The hospital was getting upset. Basically we knew what we wanted to name her but we wanted some input from the families; we wanted to include them.

We named her Aisha because of the Stevie Wonder song and because Aisha means "life" in Swahili. We're both really into heritage and culture. To us her name means life is love, just as Stevie Wonder says in the song.

> "Isn't she lovely
> Life and love are the same
> Life is Aisha
> The meaning of her name. . . ."

On her birth announcement we put the same symbol as when we got married. The *L* is for Larry, the star for Starla, and the circle for eternity, and it represents our child and possibly future children. For our children are our future = eternity.

We feel it's important for her to know her heritage, especially the African part. One thing I identified with in the series "Roots" was when Kizzy, the daughter, was taken away—I cried and cried, feeling as if Aisha's always been with us and how it must have felt.

So much of the American experience today is like the African experience but we were never conscious of it in the past. The extended family system, the reverence for children and elders. We call these Africanisms—the cultural traits that have survived slavery. Black people who were raised in this country were so isolated that they retained African beliefs and behavior without even being aware of it.

In the book *Roots,* the whole first half dealt with the African experience and black people could really identify with it because so much is similar to our way of life. The whole idea of roots is so important. Aisha has a great-great-great-aunt who lived on a plantation. Her parents were slaves. She has handed down much of the oral tradition. One of her legs is swollen and she tells how she got shot there, trying to protect the family during a race riot. She's ninety-seven now.

Those stories were passed on to us from her. I feel that family history is equally important to cultural history. My husband is making Aisha a tape of all the contributions of different peoples in America. Things that we feel will further her self-concept. We start with her song by Stevie Wonder and we have others like, "To Be Young, Gifted, and Black." We feel that if she can feel real good about herself, she'll be able to deal with other people.

I think it's important that she learn to deal with reality. I can't make my past her present. But I think I can help her when she needs it with things I've learned. I'm really an idealist but I don't see any real progress in terms of what she'll deal with as a black person. I want her to be able to deal with racism.

Sometimes I get very sad that she has to deal with it. She's so precious. You don't want anything to hurt them. The first tool of dealing with racism is a positive self-concept, the second is being there to talk with her about it, and the third is teaching her to confront it appropriately. That kind of teaching begins now and lasts forever.

I have a dream that by the time she goes to school I will be part of a private multiethnic institution and we'll have a school for children. I think institutional racism is the hardest to combat, much harder than individual racism. We think of our institutions as being powerful and right. The process of educating teachers does not include dealing with racism and racial attitudes. It's harmful to raise white children too, in a pluralistic society, without teaching them about other children. I want her to be armed with a good self-concept before she has the exposure.

About three years ago, my husband and I gave up Christmas. It was a decision about values. We don't like the materialism. My mother said Aisha needs Christmas. We said she will get it at your house. We have Kwanza, an African holiday which is similar to Chanukah. It lasts seven days and each day represents a value. The first day is the value of unity; the second, self-determination; the third, collective work and responsibility; the fourth, cooperative economics; the fifth, purpose; the sixth, creativity; and the seventh, faith. Each day you give a present but it doesn't have to be something new, it can be symbolic, a plant, a piece of fruit, and you talk about that value and what you've done with it in the last year and what you will do in the year to come. Every day you light a candle for the number of days that have already gone by.

In terms of education I want to teach her that education doesn't mean getting a piece of paper or a job. It means being an independent learner, a researcher, an analytical thinker. Even now, I read her the Black ABC's, and there's a quote: "Q is for question, the wise man's tool, who cannot ask remains a fool." I want her to question everything, even me.

I want her to understand right and wrong. I was brought up that way, but I went away from it when I got educated. I've come back to it now as I've gotten in harmony with my spiritualism. I want her to really understand that one's belief is one's behavior. Actions speak louder. We have to be the models.

I feel that kids should be raised with reality. Kids on drugs were raised to think everything was or

should be ideal. They have to be raised with a consciousness of what is: racism is, love is, sex is.

There is no objectivity. The belief in objectivity is a
value in itself.

People talk about babies. How they don't understand, how they can't really see things. She wasn't
anything like the textbooks. I guess no baby is. She
was so alert. She has been so peaceful. She seemed
so much more aware—she would sit here looking at
all these pictures of faces and I would say she was
talking to her ancestors.

They were giving her some good advice.

Retaining Mexican-American values in times of change

Emma; five children, ages 21, 19, 18, 16, 14:

In a lot of ways my values are the same as my
mother's. You can't get away from it. Mostly with the
girls. In housekeeping and having them do their own
cleaning. It's something I can remember from my
mother.

One thing that I believe in, and I've noticed a lot
of change. She believed women should do things for
men. Keep their clothes nice, do washing for them,
cook for them. She said to do this for my brothers. I
liked doing it for them and they were good to me. I
had seven brothers. I was the only girl.

In a lot of families women don't care for men anymore. I don't believe too much in women's liberation.
I like doing things for my husband. I tried to get my
girls to do things for their brothers. They don't want
to do a lot. They say they're old enough to do for
themselves. It's not the idea that they're old enough,

it's important. It's changing. I liked doing it. It's because my brothers worked from very young. They all
quit school to help the family. My mother didn't have
me work. Women stayed at home. So I helped my
brothers. I don't know if it's my girls' age that they
don't want to do it.

Something else is caring for your parents. My
mother felt very strongly. Like when they're old they
put them in nursing homes. She doesn't like things
now. I've talked to my kids about that. I asked them if
old people should be put in homes. They said no. My
daughter visited one with a friend. She came home in
tears. It would be neat if young people could visit
nursing homes and see what they're like. There are no
old-age homes in Mexico. We visited families there
and they all had grandparents living in the homes.

A lot of people have told me, "Your mother should
learn to do things for herself, like go places or phone."
I felt really hurt. If my mother becomes an invalid
she will live with me. My father had a stroke and the
doctors told us to put him in a home. My older brother
took care of him. He nursed him back to health. My
daughters told me they would never put me in a
home.

Something else is changing—when someones dies.
In Mexican families we have a wake the night before
the funeral. Now they don't take children. We always
went. I always took my kids, they cried and got over
it. They saw what happens to a person when he dies.

I pretty much knew how to take care of babies
from the time I had them. Since I was very young I
took care of babies. It was really neat when I got married because people would come and say, "You can do
everything—the cooking, the washing." I felt so good.
I had done it for so long. I tell my daughters they
won't know what to do. They don't like housework.

They joke and say they will come to me if they have
any problems. My daughters and I have always been
really close and open. I was close to my mom but not
that kind of open.

If we needed family counseling I would always talk
to the priest. But not any priest. We work in the
church—my husband and I. My husband is even a lay
priest. We get to know all the priests, we get our pick.

Once I talked to a priest. We were good friends. I
had talked about everything. When my children were
smaller they used to fight a lot. He said one family
had tried having a meeting once a week to say what
bugged them. We tried it and it worked. One thing
they felt really strongly about was when they didn't
feel good not to be bugged. If they came in, in a bad
mood, they didn't want us to ask what happened. So
we respected that.

It was so different when we were in school. Mex-
icans were not accepted. We even had a different
school. In first, second, and third grades we had to go
to a different school. In fourth there was no other
school. We had to go with the other kids. That's when
I really learned to speak English. Still we weren't
liked.

The school nurse was mean. She would tell us we
were dirty. She would say all of us had bugs in our
hair and put medicine on all of our heads and wrap
bandages around. She would only do this to the Mex-
icans. My parents never said anything. They never
went to the school. They thought what was happening to us was happening to everyone. When we were
older we told them. They couldn't have done anything. They didn't speak English.

With my kids people weren't prejudiced. They liked
school. We liked it too. Most of their friends are Anglo
kids. They want me to cook Mexican food for them.
When I was little all our friends were Mexican. At

school the others wouldn't talk to us. In seventh and eighth grades we started making friends. In high school it was different.

I like having a big family. There is always noise. Always music. We dance along with them, my husband and I. We have parties and ball games. I've really enjoyed my family. We do lots of things together. Maybe we haven't had any trouble because of the church. Right now I enjoy it the most. I haven't had any problems like other people have. Because we're strict. My husband is. I've been open. They come and tell me things that happen at parties. I don't get shocked. It wasn't that way for me. My father didn't want boys around. I ask what the boys are like, what they said.

My mother never talked about sex. It was always a secret, hush-hush. I have been very open with my children from the time they were real little. It was the way my mom was brought up. She never went to school. A lady came to the house to teach them to read. My aunt doesn't read or write. Everything I learned about sex was from friends at school. Young kids in Mexico are still very sheltered, girls especially. I've been able to talk more intimately with my girls. The boys talk more with me than with their dad, but not as intimately as the girls.

My eighteen-year-old boy tells me problems about girls. He asks me when he really needs the car. I tell him to ask his father, that he will understand. Then I go and tell my husband to understand that it's important. I feel things are very important to them. It's not less so because they're young. They're young and it's really important.

I always thought they should have their own goals. I don't like to push them into things. My nineteen-year-old is an artist. He was taking courses at college for two years. Finally he said there's no future in it.

My husband thinks he should go on. I don't think he should. It's up to him.

I don't remember what I thought when they were little. At fourteen their personalities start to show. I worry about my fourteen-year-old. He seems immature, he's the youngest. He's been sickly. He has asthma. I wonder what he'll be like when he's older.

I think it will be sad when they leave. I'm glad I started taking classes so I will have something to do when they're gone. Now they all want to stay home. I think they'll always be around. They'll have kids. Like I was with my mother. My mother always said, "Don't build too big a house, it'll seem empty when they're gone." I respect her opinions.

I never liked my kids to run around in the neighborhood when they were little, running to other people's houses, unless they had permission from the grownups. In my family we have a rule that they must tell us where they are going.

My mother's life has changed since my father died. She never went out before. Now she does. She was different with her husband. She would never joke with him like I do with mine. But they were both the heads of their families. My mother had two children in her forties. She had never been to the hospital before, she always had midwives. She was so scared. I was a little nervous when I had babies, just normally so.

I have been in this area since I was three. I will always remember when I was a child and we all lived together in Texas before we came here. All the mothers cooking—all the children to play with. I would like that now. My mother was isolated when she came here. She didn't know anyone, she couldn't speak English, or go out. Now she goes out. I had friends because I grew up here.

NOTES

1. Ann and Don Hanley, *How to Live with Your Children and Enjoy It* (San Luis Rey, Calif.: Center for Human Enrichment, 1975), p. 1.
2. Benjamin Spock, M.D., *Raising Children in a Difficult Time* (New York: W. W. Norton & Co., 1974), p. xii.
3. Ann and Don Hanley, *How to Live,* p. 66.
4. Patricia Coffin, *1, 2, 3, 4, 5, 6: How to Understand and Enjoy the Years That Count,* photographs by James Hansen (New York: Macmillan, 1972), p. 152.
5. Michael and Karen Novak, "The Family What Hath Time Wrought," *Los Angeles Times,* May 8, 1977, p. 1, Part 5.
6. Urie Bronfenbrenner, *Two Worlds of Childhood* (New York: Russell Sage Foundation, 1970), p. 116.
7. Sidney Simon, Leland Howe, and Howard Kirschenbaum, *Values Clarification* (New York: Hart Publishing Co., 1972).
8. Michael and Karen Novak, "The Family," *loc. cit.*

9. Conclusion

There is an old Sufi story that tells of a group of blind men who tried to decide what an elephant looked like through touch alone. Each one thought that the part he was feeling was the whole animal and developed a picture of elephants based on his limited experience of reality. For one man the elephant was only a fan (one ear); for another, a rope (the tail); for the third, a pillar (the leg); and so on. The men then argued about the nature of the elephant, each insisting that the part he had experienced was the reality.

Our pictures of parenthood, like those images of the elephant, tend to be focused on certain aspects of one experience to the exclusion of others. As individuals we seem to be aware of the parts of parenthood that seem most important to us and to treat them as if they were the whole.

In the West we have a preoccupation with technology, with rationality, with science, with the development and improvement of products, with analyzing, categorizing, and finding solutions. Our approach to parenting, not surprisingly, has become in some ways a reflection of these cultural preoccupations. It is not that these emphases are wrong; just that, as with the elephant's ear and tail, they have come to be mistaken for the whole.

Today, even before we become parents, we are urged to employ a kind of rationality in making decisions about having children that leaves out what might have been called a hundred years ago "the realm of the heart." We have broken parenthood down into so many parts—how to discipline, toilet train, feed, train against sexism, and love our children—that we have often lost track of the whole. We have attempted in our analysis to make parenthood a technology, a scientific process in which our actions can be measured and proved valid, though we have not quite discovered how.

In our zest for action and answers we have often forgotten what it is to be receptive. We find it difficult to relate to our children as whole people—not just to their isolated problems, feelings, potentials, or stages of development, but to them, the beings we are living with and relating to now. We have also ignored the need to be receptive to ourselves and to the answers and ideas we have within us.

Parents sometimes say, "I go by my intuition in child raising." But in Western culture we have no real definition of the word, no way to determine when intuition is operating, when our insights have real validity.

But intuition can be an important tool for parents. In learning to be receptive to our inner experience and insights, we can start to achieve a balance in our approach to parenthood. We do not have to reject the learning of valuable parental skills, the utilization of techniques that work for us, the assimilation of information on how children develop. To do so would be like throwing out the baby with the bath. But like the men exploring each part of the elephant, it is essential to be aware that these activities are only part of the whole.

We might call the part of parenting that has been neglected in the past few generations "the inner parent." The inner parent is the part of ourselves that is receptive to our own ideals, insights, and feelings but can also put them into perspective with the ideas and resources presented by the world. The *inner parent* is not a psychological term used to describe a part of the psyche. It is not to be confused with the ideal parent, the shadow parent, or any other term used to structure our personalities or behavior. It is rather a way of being, a way of approaching the world, that is more concerned with organizing our own perceptions of and attitudes toward reality than with adopting someone else's. Perhaps, most importantly, the inner parent is the part of ourselves that is capable of enjoying parenthood. It is difficult to take joy in something while we are trying to analyze it or are looking at it as a series of problems. The joy comes in just being and in the learning that takes place when we see the *process* of parenting as being important. With that perspective we can even enjoy our mistakes and our crises because they are some of our best teachers.

The inner parent is not passive. It does not stand *in contrast to* the parent who acts, analyzes, and finds answers as much as it works to put all these activities in context. If it has an opposite, it might be our stereotypes of what we as parents are or should be. Stereotypes do not grow, and the inner parent is most concerned with growth—the real learning that takes place in the long and short run of everyday experience.

The various chapters in this book should not be taken as descriptions of what the inner parent should look like: one who skillfully balances his needs with those of his child, one who is in touch with her identities or keeps a journal about her children. We mean for these processes to be taken up as tools to help you on your personal journey toward experiencing the nature of parenthood.

As you proceed on your journey in deciding how or whether to be a parent, let us make just one prescription: nurture your inner parent as wholeheartedly as you would your child. Whether you are relating to your children now or in the future or to children you meet, it will help you to make your life and the lives of others more complete.